nds for
ovement

Grounds for
Improvement

40 Great Landscaping & Gardening Projects

Dean Hill & Jackie Taylor

A Division of Sterling Publishing Co., Inc.
New York

Series Editor: Dawn Cusick
Assistant Editor: Matt Paden
Series Designer: Thom Gaines
Cover Designer: DIY Network, Stewart Pack
Contributing Writer: Susan Brill
Production: Jackie Kerr, Matt Paden
Illustrations: Dean Hill

10 9 8 7 6 5 4 3 2 1

First Edition

Published by Lark Books, A Division of
Sterling Publishing Co., Inc.
387 Park Avenue South, New York, N.Y. 10016

Text © 2007, Lark Books
Book design © 2007, Lark Books
Photography © 2007, DIY Network

Distributed in Canada by Sterling Publishing,
c/o Canadian Manda Group, 165 Dufferin Street
Toronto, Ontario, Canada M6K 3H6

Distributed in the United Kingdom by GMC Distribution Services,
Castle Place, 166 High Street, Lewes, East Sussex, England BN7 1XU

Distributed in Australia by Capricorn Link (Australia) Pty Ltd.,
P.O. Box 704, Windsor, NSW 2756 Australia

If you have questions or comments about this book, please contact:
Lark Books
67 Broadway
Asheville, NC 28801
(828) 253-0467

Manufactured in China

ISBN 13: 978-1-60059-102-0
ISBN 10: 1-60059-102-7

**For information about custom editions,
special sales, premium and corporate purchases,
please contact Sterling Special Sales Department
at 800-805-5489 or specialsales@sterlingpub.com.**

Contents

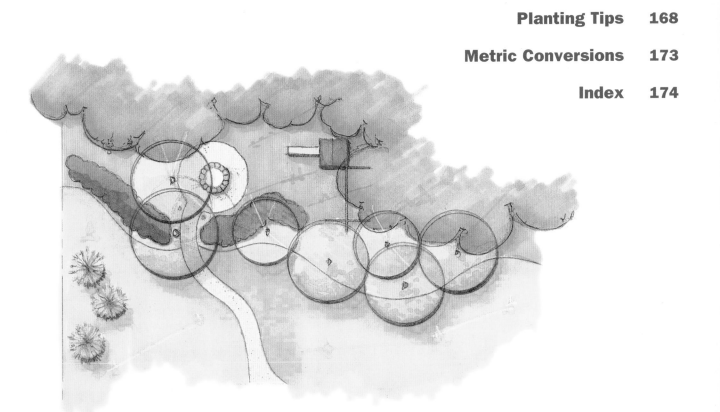

Grounds for
Improvement

Welcome to the pages that are going to help you make your dreams and ideas for your outdoor living spaces come true! The most common feedback we hear from homeowners is their surprise at how much can be done to transform those spaces in just a few days. With the proper tools, knowledge, leadership, and plenty of help, you can do a lot in a reasonably short period of time! And perhaps the most rewarding aspect for us is demystifying the process for homeowners, giving them a clear road map to follow, and watching them realize they can do this. A lot of homeowners get bogged down in fear, or they start one project and move on to something else before the first is finished–always feeling like their yard is a work in progress without a sense of completion.

If this sounds like you, read on. These projects will give you a roadmap to shop for, start, and, most of all, finish your dreams for your yard. Landscaping work is very linear—you need to follow the process from A to Z instead of jumping all over the place. We've got the A-Z (well, the 1-2-3) right here for you.

We love helping people see that they don't have to be multi-millionaires or own 40-acre estates or have large budgets to hire designers. They just need a process to define their ideas and organize them in a way that they can be incorporated into their landscape. You need to have the dream before you can build the dream! We relish the idea that if you can dream it, you can find a way to build it.

We have a lot of fun in what we do, and we think you will, too. So pick out a dream-yard project from these pages, and we'll show you how to do it yourself

Dean Hill & Jackie Taylor
Hosts of DIY Network's *Grounds for Improvement*

Grounds for Improvement

1

Patios, Porches, & Plantings

Patios and porches are a wonderful way to extend the living space of your home into the outdoors. Using design choices that complement the style and era of your house, you can create a new outdoor living space that fits in as though it's always been there. And your outdoor rooms can reflect your taste as much your indoor rooms by the materials and furnishings that you use. Then, gardens and plants are the baubles—the finishing touches that grace the whole look and tie it together. While horticulture is not the prime focus of this book, it is an integral complement to the hardscaping projects here and in every chapter.

SHADE SAIL PATIO

The lives of Cindy and her sculpture artist husband, Preston, revolve around their two children—and so does their backyard. While the large, fenced-in area was kid-friendly, no shade was available where adults could relax. Preston had created a sculpture garden for Cindy when they were expecting their first child, and now it suffered from years of neglect.

PROJECT SUMMARY

The *Grounds for Improvement* team developed a plan to create a dramatic, shady area to complement the couple's artistic style. Dean installed a set of three triangular shade sails to fly above a checkerboard patio area of pavers and tumbled green glass. In the sculpture garden, the crew trimmed and tamed overgrown plants and shrubs and reclaimed long-lost pieces of art.

BEFORE: The backyard was already a functional space because it was open and flat; however, it lacked an interesting focal point and a place to relax (below).

AFTER: The shade sail patio, complete with artistic hammock stand and checkerboard paver installation, is both dynamic and inviting (opposite page). The small sculpture garden in the corner of the yard was spruced up to further beautify the yard (above).

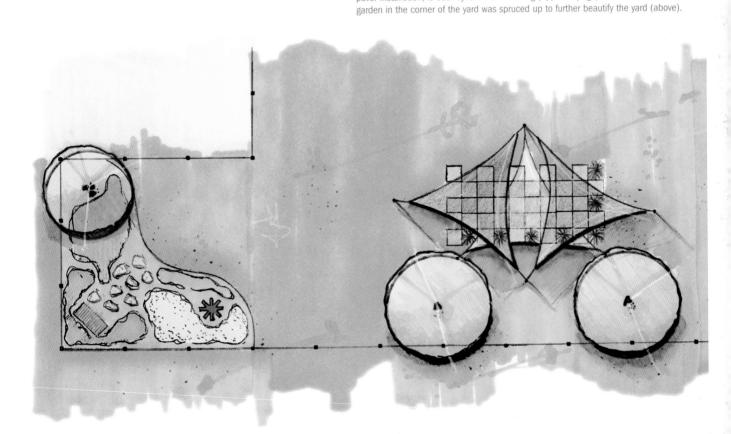

◄ BUILDING A PAVER AND TUMBLED-GLASS PATIO ►

This patio consists of a checkerboard pattern of pavers and tumbled green glass—a newly available material that adds color and texture to this artistic setting. Tumbled glass is just that—recycled glass which has been tumbled so that no sharp edges remain. You can even walk on it. It's a safe material for the yard, and when it gets wet it really sparkles and shines! You will want to rent a sod cutter for this project to reduce manual labor.

You Will Need

4 stakes	Wheelbarrows
String	Landscape fabric
Landscape marking paint	Landscape spikes
(30) 24" x 24" paver slabs	Mallet
2' level	Utility knife or scissors
Spades	Broom
Shovels	(12) 50-pound bags of tumbled glass
Rakes	60 linear feet of landscape edging
Tape measure	Reciprocating saw
Sod cutter	

SOLID GROUND FOR PAVERS

Removing the grass underneath pavers allows them to sit more securely. Pavers as large as 24x24, as in this project, can be placed directly on level soil. They are heavy enough that they will not move. Smaller pavers, however, often require a gravel base, rather than soil, to keep them in place and level.

1 Determine the area for the patio, and drive a stake into each corner of the area. Tie string between the stakes to mark the perimeter, and also tie string diagonally from the corners to find the center of the patio (and the pattern). Mark it with landscape paint. Remove the diagonal string to clear the area for work, but leave the perimeter string for reference in laying the pavers.

2 Lay out the perimeter of the patio by placing 24-inch pavers 2 feet apart over the existing sod. The sod inside the perimeter will be removed with a sod cutter, but the sod under each paver will be removed by hand since it requires more precision. Set a level across the pavers to make sure one is not higher or lower, adjusting to make them even.

3 Use a spade to cut through the sod around each paver (photo A). Then, move the pavers and use the spade to remove the sections of sod underneath (photo B). Carefully level the dirt below and return the pavers to position (photo C). Measure between the pavers, adjusting to make sure they are 24 inches apart. (You can reuse some of the pieces of sod around the base of the shade sail posts, if needed.)

4 Next, use a sod cutter to remove the sod inside the perimeter of the paver border (photo D). Sod cutters can be rented by the day at most home centers. After cutting the sod into strips, use a shovel and spade to loosen the strips underneath. Roll them up and remove them in wheelbarrows. Clean out any remaining strips of grass, and then rake the area level.

5 Place the inside rows of pavers, alternating paver positions in each row to achieve a checkerboard pattern (photo E).

6 Next, cut 2x2-foot squares of landscape fabric with a utility knife or scissors. Secure the pieces over the patches of dirt between the pavers with spikes (photo F). This will keep the glass from sinking into the ground as well as prevent weeds from growing up into the glass.

7 After the weed barrier is secured, sweep off the pavers. Then, pour the tumbled glass into the open squares (photo G), smoothing it to the height of the paver stones (photo H). Use a broom to sweep stray glass into place.

8 Install an edging strip around the patio (photo I): Use a spade to create a crevice around the perimeter, deep enough that the edging stands only ½ to 1 inch above the ground, creating a mowing or trimming edge. Set the edging into the crevice. Secure it using a mallet and the spikes provided with the edging. Use a reciprocating saw, if necessary to cut a length of edging to size.

FINISHING TOUCHES

Remove two or three additional squares of sod on the perimeter row of the patio to replace with plantings, such as the Zebra grass used in this project. Also, buy a hammock and frame for the patio or build an artistic hammock frame, as these homeowners did.

■ INSTALLING SHADE SAILS ■

This project uses three triangular shade sails, set at different heights and overlapping. The sails offer an overhead enclosure with a light, sculptural feel. For this project, be sure that your underground utility lines are marked before you dig! Rent an auger for this project to make quick work of the postholes.

A

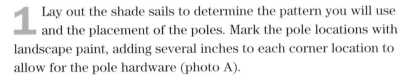

You Will Need

(3) 17' shade sails and hardware	Water source
Landscape marking paint	Scrap rebar or 2x2
Auger	Metal punch
Posthole digger	Mallet
(6) 14' posts in 4" diameter	Drill and bits
(12) #80 bags of concrete mix	9 sets of eyebolts, washers, and nuts

1 Lay out the shade sails to determine the pattern you will use and the placement of the poles. Mark the pole locations with landscape paint, adding several inches to each corner location to allow for the pole hardware (photo A).

2 Using an auger, dig the holes approximately 3 feet deep. Be sure to keep the auger level as you work, or it will begin to bog down in the dirt and start smoking (photo B). Use a posthole digger to clean out loose dirt from the holes.

B

TIPS
DIY Network
Gardening & Landscaping

TAPE IT
Don't keep measuring the hole to know how deep you've dug, instead measure 3 feet up on the auger and mark it with bright tape. When the tape is at ground level, your hole is 3 feet deep (photo at right).

CLEARING OUT A SCULPTURE GARDEN

Preston had created a sculpture garden for Cindy when they were expecting their first child, but it suffered from years of neglect—seven years, to be exact! However, it was worth resurrecting. This garden offers a great focal point from the new patio, and as Preston and Cindy learned, sculpture gardens aren't just for adults. This one also became a great place to display the kids' sculptures and handiwork.

1 Pull out the plants that you don't want. Be careful of poison ivy or other irritant plants, which may be thriving in your neglected space. It's a good idea to wear gloves, long pants, and long sleeves when doing this kind of clean up.

2 Next, trim and prune back the plants and shrubs that you want to keep. Prune aggressively to get rid of dead or gangly branches so that the energy of the plant goes into producing new growth—rejuvenation—rather than sustaining old or sprawling limbs. For instance, neglected butterfly bushes can be pruned drastically back to 6" above the ground once a year, in the spring, and will come back and flourish.

3 Then, mulch. A thick layer of mulch can keep weeds under control and give a rich look to the garden. Replant the area with a few native plants and shrubs that will thrive even without regular attention.

4 Finally—create! Even if you're not an artist, you can create your own "sculpture" garden with interesting found objects or conversation pieces. Preston and Cindy had a large piece of marble on display in their garden, which they harvested from a building being demolished. They also displayed a sculpture their five-year-old had made. Look for items that are, of course, weatherproof, and ones with visual interest, or just a great story behind them. Unleash the creativity in your kids and ask each one to find or create a piece to feature in the garden.

3 Then, set in the metal posts (photo C), angling them slightly to the outside for the shade sails, rather than precisely vertical about 10-12 degrees or according to your shade sail instructions. Hold the posts in place with hard-packed dirt, pour in dry concrete mix, and add water to set the mixture. Use a scrap of rebar to make sure water goes to the bottom of the hole.

4 Drill a hole through the poles at the desired height for the sail and install the hardware. In this project, the heights were 9, 10, and 11 feet for the three sails. Installation instructions and hardware are typically included with the shade-sail kit. The pole holes were first made with a metal punch and mallet, then drilled with a pilot bit, and finally drilled with a ½-inch bit (photo D).

5 Install an eyebolt through the hole with a washer on both sides and a nut securing it (photo E). Then clip the hook of the sail onto the eyebolt. When each sail is attached to its poles, adjust the tension on the turnbuckle of the hook to make the sails taut across.

ZEN TEAHOUSE

Homeowners Glenn and Nancy traveled extensively and fell in love with the gardens in Japan that made beautiful landscapes out of small spaces. They wanted to transform their enclosed backyard into a tranquil Japanese garden but lacked the know-how. *Grounds For Improvement* Landscape Designer Dean Hill developed a plan for their yard based on a traditional Japanese tea ceremony. He and Jackie Taylor gave the homeowners landscaping lessons with an international flair.

◤ PROJECT SUMMARY ◥

Japanese gardens often have a teahouse and a gateway or a border. This project has all of those. A cedar teahouse was first on the list for a dramatic and functional focal point for this backyard. Then, the crew built a garden gateway in the same cedar-and-fabric fashion of the teahouse, along with a simple bamboo fence. They finished off the project with an authentic Japanese garden between the walk and the teahouse. This backyard renovation was so comprehensive that everything else in the backyard was cleared out—including a trellis, some shrubs, and decorative rocks—so the work could begin on a blank slate.

BEFORE: A concrete-slab patio and minimal landscaping made the old backyard an under-utilized space in need of an update.

AFTER: With the creation of this Japanese-inspired teahouse and garden, the yard is now a relaxing and inspiring retreat.

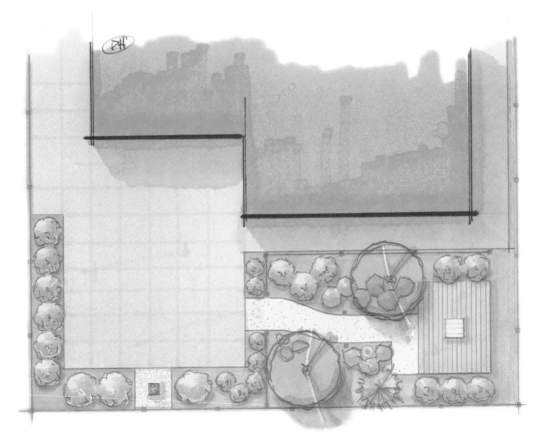

◀ CEDAR TEAHOUSE ▶

This breathtaking cedar house, while not a traditional teahouse, uses white landscape fabric and creative carpentry to provide a Japanese-style area for serving tea and enjoying the tranquility of the garden. Cedar was often used for traditional temples and other buildings in Japan because it was readily available. At one time, teahouses were made with paper walls. This teahouse imitates those traditions using cedar wood and white landscape fabric.

You Will Need

String	Water source
Rebar stakes	Joist hangers
Tape measure and pencil	2½-3" galvanized deck screws
Landscape marking paint	Miter saw
Shovels	4x4 posts
Posthole digger	2x6 cedar decking
4x4 pressure-treated posts	Reciprocating saw
Drill and bits	Hammer
3" lag bolts	2x4 boards
Socket wrench	Landscape fabric, white
2x8 cedar boards	Stapler and staples
4' or 6' level	Decorative medallion (optional)
Quick-set concrete	

1 Determine the location for the 10x8 teahouse platform, and outline it using string and rebar (photo A). In this project, the site was set several feet away from the privacy fence surrounding the yard to allow for storage and access behind the teahouse. Be sure to square the footprint of the platform with any pre-existing elements such as a privacy fence or sidewalk.

2 Mark the location for postholes with landscape marking paint (photo B). For small joists such as these 2x8s, you will also want to use center posts on each side and in the center to have a sturdy platform.

3 Use shovels and posthole diggers to dig holes for each post (photo C). Check the frostline for your region and be sure to dig below that line for postholes. In this case, the crew dug holes 18 inches deep. The posthole digger is useful for cleaning the loose soil out of holes dug with shovels, as well as a good method to dig deeply quickly by itself.

4 Attach 4x4 pressure-treated posts, cut to the depth of your postholes, to the cedar boards for the sides of the platform. Predrill holes and use 3-inch lag bolts to secure the 2x8 framing boards to the posts. Then set the boards in place into the postholes (photo D).

5 Check one side board for level. Then, making sure the corner is flush, attach the front board to the side board. Predrill holes for the lag bolts and use a socket wrench to secure the boards (photo E). Keep the boards level as you work. Continue with each side of the platform, checking for level before and after attaching each board.

6 Set the posts with quick-setting concrete and water. Use a scrap of rebar or other strong stake to work the mixture to the bottom of the post and to push out any air pockets in the cement (photo F). Make sure the mixture clings to the post in the hole. The concrete will set in several hours.

7 Continue checking the platform frame for level as the posts are set in order to make any final adjustments (photo I). Making the frame level is one of the most important details of building the structure.

8 After the concrete is dry, set joist hangers onto the frame at exactly 12-inch intervals on center. This enables you to know where to drive the deck screws when the platform boards are laid. Then, set 2x8 joists into the hangers (photo H). Make sure each joist is flush on top with the frame, and use deck screws to attach each hanger.

9 Bevel the top of four support posts for the walls. Also bevel the top pieces of the teahouse, if desired. Use a miter saw to make the cuts. When beveling posts, make 45-degree angle cuts on each side. To bevel a post to a point, start the bevel the same distance down the post as the width of the post. (For a 4x4 post, this is about 3¾ inches.) To leave a flat top, begin the cut 1 or 2 inches down the post (photo I).

10 Lay down the platform decking, measuring a 1-inch reveal, or overhang, for the board at the front edge of the platform (photo J). Set the first support post in place against the first decking board and inside the first joist. Four support posts will be erected on each corner of the platform in this manner.

11 Install the corner support posts by securing them to the joists, through predrilled holes, with lag bolts. Continue to check for plumb and level as you secure the posts.

12 Lay the second deck board in place and mark it for cutting around the posts. Use a reciprocating saw to cut out the notches. Slide the board in place and use a hammer on the edge of the plank to fit it tightly to the posts (photo K). Repeat steps 10–12 for the back posts as well.

13 Install the platform decking using galvanized or coated deck screws (photo L), fastening the boards every 12 inches to be sure to hit the joists below. To finish the edges of the deck, snap a chalk line to mark a 1-inch reveal. Use a circular saw to cut along the chalk line.

MONK MEDALLIONS

The homeowners told the story behind the medallion they used on the front piece of their teahouse. Nancy said when you go to the shrines in Japan, the monks sell little wooden plaques with motifs on them. You can write a wish on the plaque and the monks will burn it, saying that your wish has gone up to heaven. Nancy saved her favorite plaque with a black and white cat as a souvenir and used it to decorate the peak of the teahouse.

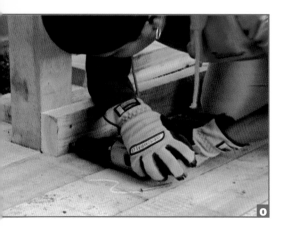

14 Mark the top pieces of the teahouse with decorative curves for cutting, in keeping with Japanese style, which uses curvilinear rather than rectangular lines. Use a jigsaw to make the cuts (photo M).

15 Secure the top pieces to the support posts, keeping the posts plumb as you work and making sure the top piece is level (photo N).

16 Attach a 2x4 board across the bottom of the support posts, against the floor of the platform (photo O). This board will hold the fabric for the wall.

17 Align the white, all-weather, landscape fabric on the side of the board facing out (photo P). Fold the edge of the fabric into a hem, and staple it onto the board.

18 Keep the fabric taut by laying it over the top beam (photo Q). Then staple the material to the top beam as well. Use a utility knife to cut off the excess at the edge of the board, this will be folded under a covering board later.

19 Repeat steps 17 and 18, overlapping additional panels of fabric to cover the width of the posts. Then, repeat steps 16–18 for the adjoining wall of the teahouse. (In this project, two sides of the teahouse were walled with fabric, closing off the view of the privacy fence but leaving the teahouse open to the walkway and garden.)

20 Use cedar 2x4s along the base and top of the fabric to cover the seam of staples (photo R). Secure the 2x4s with decking screws, keeping in mind that you may want to remove these boards in the future to replace weathered or damaged fabric.

21 Measure and mark the top front piece boards for cutting. These are tapered on one end and cut at 45-degree angles on the other end. The angled ends will be joined to form a peak. Mark another board to cut a decorative shape to mask the seam of the peak. Use a circular saw to cut the boards to size, and a jigsaw to make the curved cuts.

22 Assemble the front piece by toenailing the peak together with screws. Then place the decorative center piece over the seam, and attach it from behind with long decking screws. If desired, attach a medallion onto the center piece, as was done in this project (see sidebar page 25).

23 Raise the assembled top front piece of the teahouse and secure it to the support posts with decking screws (photo S). Keep the upright posts plumb as you work, and make sure the front piece is centered and even.

TIPS | DIY Network Gardening & Landscaping

FRESH WALLS

As the fabric panels wear over time in the elements, simply remove the boards that cover the staples, and pull off the fabric. Staple new fabric into place, and secure the 2x4s again over the seam of staples.

BAMBOO FENCE

This fence was installed along an existing sidewalk with beveled posts and rolls of bamboo fencing, which makes for simple installation.

You Will Need

Landscape marking paint	4' level
Tape measure and pencil	Quick-set concrete
Posthole digger	Water source
Miter saw	Rebar or other stake
4x4 cedar or pressure-treated posts	Bamboo fencing roll and twine

1 Mark out the area for postholes with landscape marking paint. Set the holes according to the length of the bamboo fencing, in this case 8 feet on center.

2 Dig the holes for the fence posts using posthole diggers (photo A).

3 Bevel the top of the 4x4 fence posts on all sides as for the teahouse (photo B).

4 Install the posts, checking them for level, and setting them with quick-set concrete as for the teahouse platform (photo C).

5 Attach bamboo fencing to the garden gateway and the fence posts using the twine that comes with the fencing (photo D). Align the edge of the fencing with the outer edge of the end posts so that, from the covered side, the bamboo extends across the width of the end posts.

The gateway is made of two framed panels on either side of the entrance to the garden. The panels are built with beveled posts and fabric to match the teahouse. The posts marking the entrance extend higher than the outside posts of the panels to create the sense of a "gateway."

You Will Need

Landscape marking paint	Drill and bits
Tape measure and pencil	4' level
Posthole digger	Quick-set concrete
Miter saw	Water source
4x4 cedar posts	Rebar or other stake
2x4 cedar boards	Landscape fabric, white
Circular saw	Stapler and staples
2½-3" galvanized deck screws	

1 Mark out the area for postholes with landscape marking paint according to the width of the gateway panels. Dig the postholes as for the teahouse platform.

2 Measure and mark the lumber for the gateway panels. Bevel the top of the 4x4 posts as for the teahouse. Cut 2x4s to size for the panel cross supports using a circular saw.

3 Toenail the cross supports into the posts with screws to build the frames (photo A).

4 Set the frames in place in the postholes, level them, then wrap the cross supports with fabric (photo B).

5 Attach the fabric to the gateway panels in the same manner as for the teahouse.

6 Set the posts with concrete as for the teahouse (photo C).

Simplicity is a key element in a Japanese garden. Stone accents and a sand path are just the beginning. Stylish Asian containers add color and dramatic bamboo plants cast the fine texture of leaf shadows on the teahouse fabric.

You Will Need

Spade	Landscape fabric and spikes
Metal edging with spikes	Boulders, rocks, pebbles
Mallet	Sand
Reciprocating saw or hack saw	Decomposed granite

1 Create a pathway from the gateway to the teahouse with metal edging (photo A). Use a mallet and the stakes provided by the manufacturer to secure the edging through the joints into the ground. Cut the edging to size with a reciprocating saw or hack saw.

2 Lay down landscape filter fabric on the pathway to keep the stone you will install separate from the soil (photo B). Secure the fabric with landscape spikes every few feet.

3 Place boulders in the garden beds (photo C), as well as smaller rock and pebbles (photo D). Then haul sand to the garden beds to fill around the rocks.

4 Finally, pour decomposed granite onto the pathway within the edging. Rake the granite smooth (photo E).

FINISHING TOUCHES

Fill Asian pots with hardy, clump-forming bamboo. This variety of bamboo will not send out runners and overtake the yard. Place the plants beside or behind the teahouse fabric where the sun can cast the shadow of the leaves onto the fabric. Paint wood blocks with Japanese calligraphy to decorate the posts of the teahouse, gateway, or fence.

COBBLESTONE COURTYARD

In historic Savannah, Georgia, Jody, and Kim have two annual traditions: backyard projects and Cinco de Mayo parties. From a privacy fence to a backyard deck, they've made plenty of new additions to the yard, but no single feature ties the yard together. So with a large party in the planning stages and a new baby due in just five weeks, these homeowners have turned to *Grounds for Improvement* team Jackie Taylor and Dean Hill for help transforming their backyard into a perfect environment for parties as well as relaxation. Jackie and Dean replicate the visual design elements of Savannah parks—fountains and squares—in this backyard.

◢ **PROJECT SUMMARY** ◣

In historic Savannah, river rock and cobblestones were often used as paving materials, so old-style paving bricks are in a basketweave pattern for the walkway. This project takes two separate backyard areas--a deck and a patio--and connects them visually, flowing around a small courtyard with a fountain and sitting area.

BEFORE: With a deck and a privacy fence, this yard had a good start but lacked any style.

AFTER: The courtyard adds unmistakable style to this yard and home, and provides a tranquil space to relax or entertain guests.

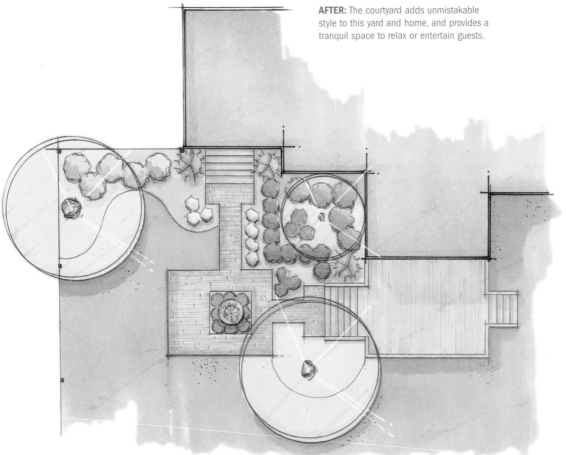

◄ DECK-TO-DECK PAVER WALKWAY ►

The cobblestone path allows easy circulation between the back door, patio, and deck, and the fountain creates a focal point that ties them all together. You will want to rent a compact utility loader for this project to easily move the heavy pavers and gravel on site. Renting a laser transit will also simplify the job of ensuring the walkway is level, and a plate compactor is needed to tamp the gravel and walkway.

You Will Need

Landscape marking paint	2x4 board for screeding
Tape measure	300 square feet of Holland stone pavers (2⅜" thick)
Laser transit level	
Shovels	(20) 8' sections of paver edging
Rakes	1 box of timber spikes
Wheelbarrows	Mallet
5 tons of base gravel	PVC pipe
18" plate compactor	Hand tamp
1.5 tons of concrete sand	

1 To determine the fountain location, mark the center point of the deck stairway and the center point of the patio walkway. Center the area for the fountain on these lines, so that it will be the focal point from each direction.

2 Use a laser transit to check the elevation of the ground at the base of the brick patio. Add or remove soil as needed to make the project area completely level. Then, determine the width and length of the walkway and mark it with landscape marking paint, outlining the area for the walkway and the area for the fountain in the center (photo A).

3 Next, determine how much to excavate the area. Allow for a 4-inch course of gravel, a 1-inch course of sand, and the thickness of the brick. In addition, if your new walkway is going to meet existing steps from a patio or deck, make sure the top of the walkway is the same distance from the last step as the other steps are to each other (photo B); otherwise people will easily trip on the stair. Then excavate the area to an even depth with shovels (photo C) while continuing to check for level throughout. A laser transit will simplify this step significantly. (See "Using a Laser Transit," page 37)

4 Use wheelbarrows to haul gravel for the excavated site. Spread a 4-inch base of gravel evenly over the area, raking it smooth, and tamping it down with a plate compactor (photo D). Check the gravel base for level with the laser transit.

5 To lay a 1-inch course of sand over the gravel, first lay down lengths of 1-inch diameter metal pipe along the length of the graveled walkway (photo E). Pour the sand over the gravel, between the pipes, and smooth it out with a rake. To level the sand to a 1-inch depth, run a 2x4 board down the poles (photo F), displacing any extra sand and filling in the low points. This leveling of the sand base is a process known as screeding. After sand is filled and leveled in one area, slide the poles to the next section to repeat the process. Fill in the depressions in the sand left by the poles, being careful not to walk on the leveled sand.

TIPS DIY Network
Gardening & Landscaping

BUYING SAND

Use concrete sand, sold in gravel and stone stores, for paver foundations because the granules are coarser than fine mortar sand, letting it pack down but still allowing moisture and water to drain away from the path.

BURYING ELECTRICAL LINES

Before installing the fountain, determine where your electrical lines (and any irrigation lines) for the fountain will run. Bury a length of PVC pipe in a trench under the pavers to serve as a sleeve for the electrical cords: Brush away the sand in the area for the PVC sleeve, then dig a shallow trench with your hands in the stone base for the pipe (photo below). Seal the ends of the pipe with duct tape to keep sand and gravel from clogging them. Bury the pipe with gravel, and use a hand tamp to level the area. Reinstall the sand before putting the pavers in place on top. When the paving process is complete and the fountain is in place, remove the tape from the pipe ends and thread the fountain pump cords through the pipe to an electrical outlet.

6 Before laying the path, mark the center point of the entrance to the path—in this case, a stoop. Then, place bricks on either side of this point, and work the pattern out from there, staying within the walkway borders and always on a screeded path (photo G). If you will place a fountain in the courtyard, prepare a sleeve under the patio bricks to carry the wiring before completing the brickwork. (See "Burying Electrical Lines," left.)

7 With the pavers in place, now add metal edging to keep them from shifting. Use timber spikes to hold the edging in place (photo H), creating an attractive border between the stone and surrounding flower beds.

8 Brush sand over the walkway to fill in any cracks (photo I). Then, work the plate compactor over the walkway to seat the bricks securely in place (photo J).

USING A LASER TRANSIT

A laser transit determines level and also indicates how deep to excavate an area. The transit sits on a tripod and emits a laser beam that is picked up by a receiver, which is mounted on a graduated stake. To use the transit to excavate, set the tripod at one edge of your project area. Take the receiver to another edge of the area. With the stake resting on the ground, slide the receiver up the number of inches on the graduated stake that you want to excavate. The distance you move up on the stake is the distance you will excavate into the ground. For the walkway, you will excavate at least 7¾ inches in order to lay a course of gravel, a course of sand, and allow for the thickness of the brick. If your walkway will meet an existing stair, you may need to excavate further. In this project, the rise from the walkway to the bottom stair was 5½ inches to match the rise of the rest of the stairs. To determine how deep to excavate the ground, Dean measured from the 5½-inch mark at the base stair to the top of the patio floor. The measurement was 3 feet 9 inches. Then, he moved the transit up 7¾ inches—the depth of the pathway courses—to find the level of the excavation. The total measurement was approximately 4 feet 5 inches. He set this point on the transit. Then, the transit receiver could be moved around the area and it would sound an electronic alert if the site was too low or high in depth during the digging process. The display on the transit shows when it registers level. Be sure to take multiple measurements within the project space in order to level the entire area.

◄ INSTALLING A FOUNTAIN ►

The fountain visually connects the side patio to the back deck and is the focal point of the backyard. A three-tier Italian fountain was used in this project creating a dramatic, old-world look and a soothing sound.

You Will Need

Paver stones	Plastic plug
2' level	Plumber's putty
Italian three-tier fountain with pump and cables	Extension cord, if needed

1 Place a large paver where the fountain will sit and adjust it for level (photo A).

2 Set the fountain pedestal and the basin on the paver. Thread the pump cables through to the bottom of the pedestal (photo B), following the manufacturer's instructions. If desired, run the water hose and electrical cord under the patio as described in the sidebar on page 36 "Burying Elecrical Lines."

3 With the pump in place, seal the hole in the pedestal with a plastic plug (photo C). Put into place the remaining fountain tiers and hoses, sealing them with plumber's putty (photos D and E).

4 Plug in the fountain, fill it with water, and start the pump to check the water flow.

FINISHING TOUCHES

Use shrubs and plants to create a park-like atmosphere around the walkway and fountain. In Savannah, pine straw is used as a natural-looking mulch in planting beds and is readily available across the U.S. Place ornate metal and wood benches along the walkway as well.

PARTY-TIME PATIO

Joel and Jefferson are homeowners in Los Angeles with a patio that does not adequately serve the four bachelors living there, who frequently entertain friends. A bag of potting soil holds down a flapping piece of metal on the roof, a brick barbecue island has a built-in grill that isn't safe for grilling, and the patio beside the backyard swimming pool just isn't reaching its potential.

◀ **PROJECT SUMMARY** ▶

Using metal for functionality as well as visual impact gives an industrial and modern feel to this very hip renovation. After demolishing a defunct, built-in barbecue island, the remodel includes installing a metal roof, building an industrial-style countertop, and constructing wall screens with perforated sheet metal.

BEFORE: This house full of bachelors needed more than just a clean up to make the most of the old pool-side patio.

AFTER: With the help of Jackie and Dean, the patio now has a modern feel, and it's also more functional for entertaining. The unique metal screens and new plantings provide a hip backdrop for any gathering.

REMOVING A BARBECUE ISLAND

If gas or electricity are connected to your island, make sure the gas is shut off from a main and electricity is turned off at the breaker before you proceed. Also assess whether any support posts for the roof are built in to the island, as they were in this project.

You Will Need

Safety goggles and gloves	4x4 support beams
Sledge hammers	Wheelbarrow
Reciprocating saw	

1 After gas to the grill is turned off, remove the grill from the island.

2 Wearing safety goggles and gloves for protection, use sledge hammers to demolish the island (photo A). Be sure that you swing with your back to the house, away from any windows and doors. Keep your hands and feet away from the brick as you work—the material is heavier than it looks and could cause injury when it falls.

3 Before you cut out a load-bearing post, wedge another piece of lumber under the roof for support (photo B). Then, use a reciprocating saw to cut the post away from the island (photo C). In this case, electrical wire was run externally along the post from the ceiling, so before removing the post completely, the wiring needed to be detached.

4 Use wheelbarrows to haul away the accumulating debris as you take breaks from the demolition. Then, after the demolition is completed, install support posts to replace those that were taken out.

◀ INSTALLING A METAL PATIO ROOF ▶

In this project, old opaque sheeting was cracked and loose from wind and weather. This material could not bear weight, so the work of removing it was done from ladders. Then, the old material was replaced with new galvanized metal sheeting. Be sure to check the strength of your roof before climbing up to work.

You Will Need

▶ Hammer	▶ Shovels or broomsticks
▶ Crow bar	▶ Galvanized metal roofing
▶ Drill with bits	▶ Coated metal fasteners
▶ Ladder	▶ Tape measure
▶ Safety goggles and gloves	

1 Use hammers and crow bars to pull out the nails of the old roof sheeting (photo A), or use a drill in reverse to back out old screws. Then, roll the material back, and move the ladders to the inside of the joists to continue working. Be sure to wear safety goggles and gloves for demolition like this.

2 Push the sheeting loose from underneath, using shovels and broomsticks or any long implements. Roll up the old material and haul it away.

3 Lay the sheets of galvanized metal roofing in place (photo B) using a tape measure to gauge an even overhang. Galvanized metal comes in a variety of colors, with trim and other accessories available as well. Silver was used in this project to create a simple, industrial motif for the patio.

4 Use coated metal fasteners to attach the sheeting about every 12 inches into the canopy frame (photo C). Make sure to place the fasteners in between the ribs of the metal panel, not into them.

5 Secure subsequent sheets of metal roofing according to the manufacturer's instructions. With this metal, each sheet overlapped by one rib. Secure one edge over another with fasteners. Lay the last metal panel in place and cut to fit with tinsnips or electric shears.

◣ BUILDING A DIAMOND-PLATED METAL COUNTERTOP ◢

"Diamond plate" is the pattern stamped onto sheet metal for use on this table. The countertop is made of exterior plywood with a sheet metal veneer and galvanized metal legs.

You Will Need

Diamond-plated sheet metal	Drill and bits
¾" plywood	Socket wrench
Tape measure and pencil	½" hex bolts
2' or 4' level	½" stainless steel screws and washers
Circular saw	2x4 scrap
Safety goggles and gloves	
Galvanized metal table legs	

1 Lay the metal over the plywood to measure the plywood to size (photo A), allowing for a slight overhang of ¾ inch of the metal on each side. This will allow the metal to wrap down the edge of the board. Mark the plywood across and use a level or straight-edge to join the marks to create a cutting line.

2 Use a circular saw to make the cuts (photo B). Be sure to wear safety goggles and gloves when using a saw.

3 Position the metal table legs on the plywood (photo C). The legs are made of standard galvanized pipe with a T-couple to hold the cross bar, extensions for the legs below the cross bar, a flange to attach the legs to the countertop, and endcaps that can be adjusted for height to make the table level (photo D).

4 With the legs in position, predrill holes in the wood through the leg mounts (or flanges).

5 Use a socket wrench to install hex bolts, also called hex cap screws or machine bolts. They will provide a tight grip on the countertop. Turn the table on its legs to install the veneer.

6 Lay the metal sheet over the plywood, keeping an even ¾ inch overhang on all sides (photo E). Use stainless steel screws and washers to tack the corners down on the top of the table (photo F), smoothing the metal down the length of the table again after installing each screw to take out any ripples or wrinkles.

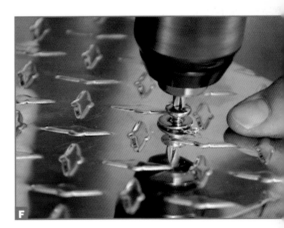

TIPS
DIY Network
Gardening & Landscaping

MARKING WITH PRECISION
Dean marks his measurements with a V-shape mark, where the point of the V is at the exact increment on the tape measure. This allows greater precision than a single hash mark would provide in drawing a cut line later.

7 When the top corners are secured, tap a 2x4 along the edge of the countertop, bending the metal to the plywood. To make the job easier, bend the metal over the short ends of the table first (photo G). Secure the corners to the plywood edge with stainless steel screws and washers. Use the 2x4 along the long edge of the plywood as well. Finish the corners by cutting a 45-degree angle to the corner and folding the edge like wrapping paper. Then screw the metal corners down on the long sides of the plywood as well.

BUILDING METAL SCREENS

These screens can help obscure or just break up long, bare masonry walls with a cool, clean look. The screens are built with perforated sheet metal and pressure-treated lumber, which is weather, termite, and fungus resistant. Sheet metal is sold in different patterns and thicknesses. Before starting, dig up any unwanted shrubs and foliage along the wall to help determine the size and position you need for your screens.

You Will Need

Miter saw	Perforated metal screen
4x4 pressure-treated posts	Landscape marking paint
Speed square and pencil	Posthole digger
Tape measure	Shovel
2x4s	4' level
Circular saw	Quick-set concrete
1" trim	Water source
2" galvanized screws	Rebar or other stake
Drill and bits	

1 Use a miter saw to bevel the top of the pressure-treated 4x4 posts. (For details on beveling, see page 24, step 9.)

2 Use a speed square to mark the posts for cutting (photo A). Then mark 2x4s to size for the horizontal boards of the frame, which will hold the metal screen. Use a circular saw to make the cuts.

3 Measure and cut to size 1-inch trim pieces for the front and back of the frame of the screen, including an extra vertical piece for the center back of the screen. Install the trim on the posts where the screen will be positioned (photo B). Secure it driving 2-inch screws in at an angle—called toenailing.

4 Secure the 2x4s to the 4x4s by toenailing 2-inch screws into the corner joints as well (photo C). Install 1-inch trim onto the 2x4s, tacking it flush with front (photo D, next page).

5 Install two sheets of perforated metal so the material will support itself in the screen (photo E). Install more 1-inch trim on the other side of the metal screen to hold it in place (photo F), using trim in the center of the screen to give extra stability (photo G).

6 Use 2-inch screws to secure the edge trim over the metal, and also screw through the center of the metal panel into the trim behind (photo H).

7 Measure and mark the location for the postholes with landscape marking paint. Then use post-hole diggers to dig the holes for the screen, or multiple screens.

8 Set the screen in place and check it for level (photo I). Adjust the soil beneath the posts to achieve level.

9 Set posts in place with quick-set concrete and water (photo J). Make sure that the mixture gets down to the bottom of the hole—a scrap of rebar makes a good poker for this purpose.

FINISHING TOUCHES

Repainting the canopy posts and selecting the right planters can do wonders for a patio facelift. The planters in this project were metal fused to fiberglass, which will patina like any metal but is extremely lightweight for easy portability. The crew used horsetail and umbrella grasses to complement the modern look of the containers. And, finally, nothing beats an indoor/ outdoor TV for party central. This one was mounted on a pole, rather than the wall, to allow a greater turning radius for the screen.

TRAVERTINE TILE PATIO

Susan and Tom recently renovated a 19th-Century home in historic Charleston, South Carolina. They yearned to transform the space outside their new French doors into an area to entertain and dine al fresco. The *Grounds for Improvement* team arrived with a plan to help them do just that.

◢ **PROJECT SUMMARY** ◣

Jackie Taylor and Landscape Designer Dean Hill showed these homeowners how to build an elegant travertine tile patio for entertaining and dining. They also constructed a cedar screen to cover up an unsightly air conditioning unit, installed some new planting beds, and added a decorative wall fountain to complete the elegant transformation.

BEFORE: These homeowners had just removed a concrete koi fish pond from their yard and needed help turning the area into a place to entertain and dine outside.

AFTER: This contemporary travertine stone patio and cedar screen transformed the bare, problem side yard into an elegant area for wining and dining.

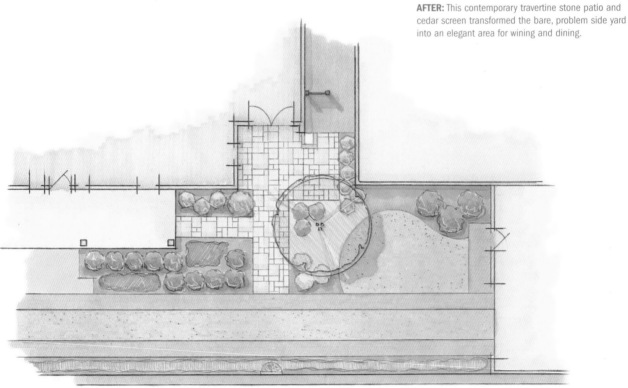

◣ BUILDING A PATIO ◢

The tiles for this project are travertine—a morphed limestone that can be used either indoors or outdoors and remains cool even in the sun. It's also maintenance-free. It has twice the strength of concrete but can be cut using a wet-table masonry saw. Aluminum edging was also used—a great choice for a patio because it's rustproof, non-corrosive, and bends easily for simple installation. You will want to rent a laser transit for this project in order to excavate and install a level base for the patio.

You Will Need

Landscape marking paint	(2) 1"-diameter poles for screeding
Shovels	2x4 board
Wheelbarrow	270 square feet of paver tiles
Tape measure and pencil	Mallet
Laser transit	Wet table masonry saw
Rakes	Safety goggles and gloves
3.5 cubic yards of base drain gravel	96 linear feet of paver-restraint edging
Plate compactor	1 box of landscape spikes
1.5 cubic yards of masonry sand	¼" sheet plywood

1 Use landscape marking paint to outline the area for the new patio. Use shovels and a wheelbarrow to remove any plants or sod in the outlined area (photo A).

2 With a laser transit, determine the elevation, or height, of the patio. This tool will show how deep to dig out the area for a level base. The depth needs to accommodate a 4-inch layer of gravel, a 1-inch layer of sand, and 1¼-inch-thick tiles—a total of 6¼ inches. Make sure the finished patio elevation is lower than the patio door so that water drains away from the door.

3 Escavate the area with shovels, removing the soil. Check for level around the excavated area with the laser transit, and dig or rake out any excess soil. (For more information, see "Using a Laser Transit," page 37.)

4 Lay down a 4-inch layer of gravel (photo B). This is a good base for a patio because it will pack down firmly, yet allow adequate drainage. Rake out the gravel evenly. Then, tamp it down with a plate compactor, using several passes. Use the laser transit to check again for level, and rake out any high areas or fill in the low ones.

5 Disperse a 1-inch layer of sand over the base gravel: Lay out 1-inch-diameter poles on the gravel layer and pour sand around them. Use a 2x4 to screed the sand over the poles until it is smooth (photo C). This method ensures that the sand course is even and level. It's very important not to walk on the sand after it has been screeded.

6 Once a few feet have been screeded, remove the poles (photo D). Carefully smooth sand into the gaps where they were. Move the poles into position for screeding the next area.

INSTALLING A SPLASHWALL

If you have a downspout inside the designated patio area, build a splash wall around it using decorative rocks. That way, the excess water will not flow directly onto your patio. It also allows the patio to be any height without disrupting the elevation of the drain. Rake any gravel away from the area, put down mortar as a base, and set the decorative rock in the mortar. This simple shield will protect your patio from flooding and send water down the drain instead.

BEFORE

AFTER

7 Arrange the paver tiles on the screeded sand in the pattern you desire. The tiles used in this project were made in 8-inch increments, so the crew used a random pattern of small and large tiles (photo E). Secure the tiles in place, using a mallet (photo F). Continue to screed additional areas of sand, laying tile as you go.

8 The last row of tiles may need to be cut to size. To do this, position each tile in place and mark off the area that needs to be cut (photo G). Use a masonry wet saw to cut the tile to size (photo H)—be sure to use safety goggles and gloves while using the saw.

9 Next, install the edging around the patio. At the edge of the patio tile, dig away the sand layer to expose the gravel base. Rest the edging on the gravel, and secure it by driving spikes through the holes provided on the edging (photo I) with a mallet. Repeat this around the perimeter of the patio. The edging will prevent any horizontal movement of the tiles.

10 To compact the surface, first throw handfuls of sand across the tiles (photo J). This will help lock them into place when compacting. Then, with a ¼-inch sheet of plywood protecting the tile surface, make several passes with a plate compactor over the entire patio. Move the plywood as you finish each section so the compactor does not contact the tile surface.

TIPS
DIY Network
Gardening & Landscaping

WET SAW SAFETY

When using a masonry wet saw, use only gentle pressure to push the table through and let the saw do the work.

◗ BUILDING A CEDAR SCREEN ◗

This screen is made of 1-x6-inch vertical cedar planks covering a cedar frame, and it attaches to the walkway rather than to the house, with masonry anchors.

You Will Need

Tape measure and pencil	Drill and bits
(3) 4" x 4" x 8' cedar posts	Brad nailer
(25) 1" x 6" x 8' cedar planks	2 masonry fasteners with plates
(5) 2" x 4" x 8' cedar	Masonry bit
Safety goggles and gloves	4' level
Circular saw	Lug bolts
2½" deck screws	Socket wrench

1 First, determine the height of the screen and use a tape measure to mark the boards and planks for cutting. Wearing safety goggles and gloves, use a circular saw (or chop saw) to cut the boards to length.

2 Use a work table or flat surface to assemble the frame for the screen. Measure several inches up from the bottom of each 4x4 post to mark the low point for the face boards of the screen (photo A). (The screen needs clearance from the ground so the wood does not soak up excess water after a hard rain.)

3 To attach the 2x4s to the posts to finish the frame, lay 1x6 planks, parallel to the posts and beneath the 2x4s. This will inset the 2x4s by 1 inch as you secure them to the end posts, allowing room for the 1x6 planks on the face to be flush with the posts (photo B). Attach the 2x4 horizontal boards to the posts with 2½-inch deck screws, countersinking each in at an angle as you go.

4 Flip the frame over, and position the cedar planks vertically on the frame. Then, use a brad nailer to secure the planks to the 2x4s (photo C).

5 Measure the position for the screen on the walkway. Mark the locations for the fasteners to drill, and then, using a masonry bit, drill into the walkway. Be sure to go completely through the brick, or other surface material, and into the concrete pad. Insert the first anchor (photo D) into the walkway, add on the plate, and tighten it down. Do the same for the other post anchor.

6 With the bases ready, set the screen in place, fitting each end post into its base. Check the screen for level, shimming the post or adjusting the height of the anchor as needed. Use a socket wrench to secure it to the anchors with lug bolts to finish (photo E).

FINISHING TOUCHES

Build new planting beds or add fresh mulch to existing beds in the patio area. If you have a dining area on your patio, as Susan and Tom do, include some large potted plants as well for ambiance. And, speaking of ambiance, a wall fountain is another great addition to the patio. The fountain this crew installed had three components: a base, a basin, and a pump—easy installation for a very dramatic effect. A great visual focal point for any patio, a fountain also creates a peaceful, soothing atmosphere with the sound of falling water.

TIPS DIY Network
Gardening & Landscaping

THE COLOR OF DUST
When drilling through a brick walkway to anchor the screen, watch the color of the dust that the drill brings up. When the color changes from the brick red to the white of the concrete below, you know you've hit the concrete.

SCREENED PORCH

Bill and Angie have a growing family and a beautiful pool in the backyard. But these homeowners often worry about the safety of their children, since there is no barrier between the door of their house and access to the pool. The view of the backyard is also obscured by a built-in bench on the porch. The family has no place to store the kids' toys outside so the area is always a mess. *Grounds for Improvement* Landscape Designer Dean Hill devised a plan to keep the kids safe and provide some outside storage for their toys.

◀ PROJECT SUMMARY ▶

Jackie Taylor and Dean Hill helped these homeowners screen in their back porch and add a locking door to keep the children inside when necessary. They also built outdoor storage bins, which double as benches, to house everything from pool equipment to children's toys.

BEFORE: An open porch and backyard created constant worry for this family with small children.

AFTER: Removing a built-in bench and screening the porch not only provided safety, but a nice view of the backyard from the house as well.

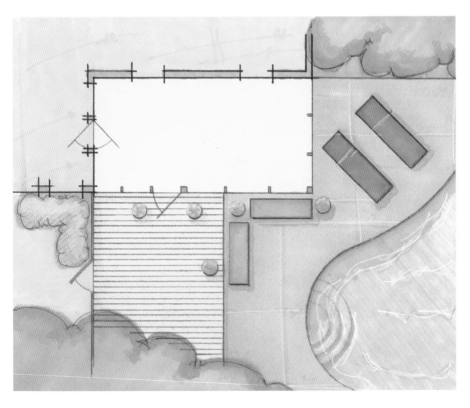

◄ INSTALLING SCREEN ►

This porch enclosure is made with a cedar frame using 2x6s for the framing structure and 2x4s for the studs. Horizontal boards are installed for extra reinforcement and also provide a natural deterrent to keep children from running through the screen. The screening system used in this project includes base strips and spline to secure the screen to the studs, and caps to cover the base strips for a finished look. The materials listed are for a 250-square-foot space.

You Will Need

Hammer or mallet	Safety goggles and gloves
Pry bar	Drill and bits
Reciprocating saw	2' or 4' level
1x6 cedar planks	Screen kit with base strips, spline, capping strips, and screening
3" galvanized deck screws	
Tape measure and pencil	Spline tool
(6) 2" x 6" x 12' cedar	1" galvanized screws
(6) 2" x 6" x 8' cedar	Utility knife
(8) 1" x 6" x 8' cedar	Tin snips, heavy duty scissors, or pruning shears
Miter saw	32" screen door with hardware

TIPS
DIY Network
Gardening & Landscaping

PREDRILL CEDAR
Cedar is a soft lumber, so pre-drill the holes for screws to avoid any splitting.

1 Clear everything from the deck, including any posts that may be in the way of the new framing. Use a reciprocating saw to remove unneeded posts, cutting them even with the deck of the porch (photo A). In this project, the crew took out some casing work around the corner post that was in the way of the framing. They replaced it with 1x6 cedar planks because of cedar's natural resistance to weather and insects (photo B).

2 Measure the area to be framed (photo C), mark the lumber for cutting, and use a miter saw to cut the boards. Always be sure to wear safety goggles when operating this type of heavy machinery.

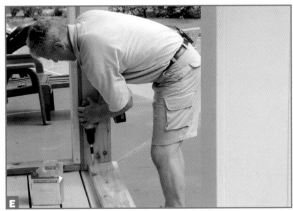

3 Pre-drill holes into the frame (photo D), and use 3-inch decking screws to secure the cedar frame boards to each section of the porch, including a bottom piece, two side pieces, and a top piece (photo E).

4 Mark the locations for studs on the bottom piece of the frame (photo F), setting the marks an equal distance apart in all of the frames—this project set them 40 inches apart to allow room to attach the 48-inch screen without stretching it.

TIPS | DIY Network
Gardening & Landscaping

CUTTERS AND BUILDERS
One way to make this kind of work go faster is to have a building crew and a cutting crew so the building crew can work continuously as the cutting crew provides the materials.

5 Measure the height needed for the studs, mark the boards for cutting, and use a miter saw to cut them (photo G). Secure the studs to the framing by driving screws in at an angle—a technique called toenailing (photo H). Make sure the studs are flush on the outside with the cedar framing to give your screen a smooth finish.

6 Build an opening for the new screen door that is ¼-inch larger than the dimension of your door all the way around. Install a header for the door, checking it for level, and fastening it to the studs with wood screws. In this project, a block was added above the door header, against the wall of the house, to provide a nailing surface for the screen (photo I).

7 The last step for framing is to install horizontal boards about 24 inches high (photo J). Hold the board in place, check for level, and then toenail the board into the stud.

TIPS
DIY Network
Gardening & Landscaping

TOENAILING

When using a toenailing technique, it's important to have the correct angle and use long enough nails or screws to get a good "bite" into the second piece of wood. Toenailing is driving a nail (or screw) in at an angle.

8 To install the screens, apply base strips to the exterior face of the framing. Install the top strip first, then the bottom strip, then butt-join them with the side strip on the vertical frame boards. Use tin snips, heavy-duty scissors, or even pruners to cut the base strips. Attach them to the frame boards with 1-inch galvanized screws, which are weather resistant (photo K).

9 Next, lay the screen over the base strips, starting at the top. Leave overhang on each side (photo L) to allow for fitting. Position a length of spline over the channel in the base strip (photo M). Spline is a ribbed rubber cord that fits into a track to hold the screen in place. Use a spline tool to work the spline into the track (photo N), holding the screen and spline taut as you go. As the spline is pressed in, it pulls the screen material taut. Cut off any excess length of spline at the end of a track (photo O).

10 Next work spline into the grooves down each side of the frame (photo P). For the bottom edge, cut the screen from the roll and secure it with spline to the base strip. Then neatly trim the screen and spline ends close to the spline line with a utility knife or scissors.

11 Apply the cap piece to the base strips. It snaps into the same track that holds the spline and screen. Trim the cap piece to fit as needed using tin snips or pruning shears. Then, use a mallet to secure it. Protect the cap piece by using a block of wood or other surface between the cap piece and the mallet (photo Q).

12 Finally, install a locking, pre-fabricated door according to the manufacturer's instructions with the hardware provided.

TIPS DIY Network
Gardening & Landscaping

KEEPING SCREEN IN PLACE

Keep the screen on its roll as you install it onto the frame. The weight of the roll at the bottom of the frame will hold the screen material still and keep it from flapping in the wind as you work with it.

These storage boxes are simple to build with cedar and treated lumber; 2x4s make up the frame with 1x12 cedar planks on the sides and pressure-treated plywood on the bottom to protect from moisture. The lid is attached with piano hinges, which are safe for use around children. The boxes can stay open during playtime or be kept closed and covered with cushions to provide extra seating.

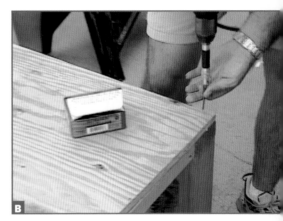

You Will Need

- 2" x 4" x 8' cedar
- ¾" x 4' x 8' pressure-treated plywood
- 1" x 12" x 8' cedar
- 2" x 2" x 8' cedar for decoration
- Circular saw
- Wood nails
- 2½" deck screws
- Drill or driver and bits
- (2) 60" brass piano hinges
- (2) 20" x 60" patio cushions (optional)
- (6) 18" all-weather pillows (optional)

1 Determine the dimensions of your box and measure and cut 2x4 cedar lumber to size. Build a simple box frame structure using wood nails (photo A).

2 Measure and cut the plywood to fit the bottom of the box and attach it with 2½-inch deck screws (photo B).

3 Measure and cut 1x12 cedar boards for the sides of the box and the lid. Attach the sides with 2½-inch deck screws. Attach the lid with a piano hinge.

4 Cut and attach decorative 2x2 wood pieces to the outside of the box if desired.

FINISHING TOUCHES

Use patio cushions and all-weather pillows on top of the boxes for seating, if desired. Plant annuals or mums around the screened porch or in urns near the storage box benches.

2

Water Features, Walkways, & Walls

Water features create ambiance and provide a great focal point for a backyard, while walkways and walls help define and connect different areas of the yard. In one project in this chapter, you'll see how a walled courtyard set apart the side yard from the front of the house and created an intimate outdoor room in a previously wasted space. To create circulation and flow in your own yard, you'll find a variety of ideas for walkways in this chapter, as well as throughout projects in the rest of the book.

If you're contemplating a water feature, consider maintenance factors. Fountains are the recent trend because of their low maintenance requirements and typically easy installation. Ponds and waterfalls, on the other hand, may have irresistible appeal but their high maintenance requires a truly committed water-feature aficionado.

FRONT YARD WATERFALL

Jeff and Melanie bought a house with an old pond in the front yard. Both of them loved the idea of a pond and had collected mountain stones over the years to accent such a feature, but the pond was overgrown and not working. *Grounds for Improvement* Landscape Designer Dean Hill created a plan to take out the old pond and expand the area with a new pond, complete with a waterfall.

◀ PROJECT SUMMARY ▶

A water feature can add interest and ambiance to any yard. In this case, the owners had been preparing for years—collecting rocks and boulders from their travels with the plan to have a waterfall. This waterfall was built in the front yard for a very dramatic effect.

BEFORE: The old pond could barely be seen beneath the foliage of the overgrown planting bed.

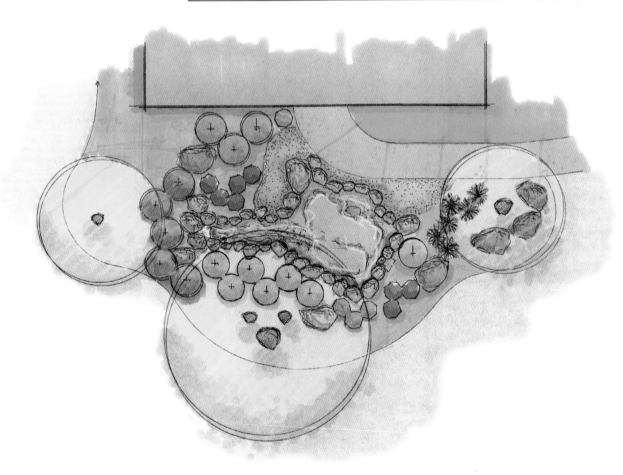

AFTER: Adding this great water feature (left) and sprucing up the surrounding bed has brought a taste of the great outdoors to the front yard.

◢ BUILDING A WATERFALL AND POND ◣

If you're replacing an old pond, be sure to clean up and organize the rocks and save any desired plants to use for the new water feature. The two components of this system are a waterfall unit and a skimmer. The water pump sits in the skimmer, in the pond where the water collects. The waterfall unit sits on the top of the water feature to pour out water over the cascading rock structure. This waterfall uses two layers to contain the water--a pool liner and an underlayment that protects it.

You Will Need

Screwdriver	Gardening clippers
Shovels	8' x 11' pond waterfall kit
Wheelbarrows	1 ton of 6" to 24" boulders
Landscape marking paint	½ ton 1½" to 2" gravel
Hose	½ ton ½" to ¾" gravel
Tarps	4 cubic yards hardwood mulch
Gloves	Silicone sealant

1 Plan out the space for your water feature, making it visible from key areas—the porch, the doorway, and the sidewalk, in this case. Mark out the area for the water feature with landscape marking paint (photo A). Outline the perimeter of the water feature, and also mark where the falls and skimmer will be located.

2 Dig the first "shelf" for the waterfall using a shovel and a pick axe, making sure to dig deep and wide enough. Also, dig out a space for the skimmer (photo B), making sure it sits level.

3 Before digging further, connect the waterfall unit to the skimmer with the hose provided. Run a bead of silicone around the outside of the hose before inserting it into the waterfall unit (photo C). This will create a seal. Then screw the water-tight coupler onto the hose to keep it in place.

4 Continue digging, creating the second shelf for the water feature, burying the hose as you go (photo D). Make a level space for the waterfall unit basin to sit.

5 Install the underlayment before installing the pond liner. This will keep rocks and roots from damaging the water feature. Make sure to cover the entire area—bottom and shelves—with the underlayment (photo E).

6 Lay the liner over the underlayment. Fitting the liner is very important. It's like a pie crust—everything else for the pond will go inside of it. Press down on the liner and underlayment to make sure they fit tightly to the ground (photo F). Wrinkles in the liner don't matter at this point; after stones are brought in, the liner will smooth out.

7 Attach the liner to the skimmer. First, trace the opening of the skimmer onto the liner, and then use a utility knife to cut the liner (photo G, next page). Put silicone sealant around the edge of the skimmer (photo H, next page) and place the liner on top. Use sealant around the edge of the skimmer plate as well, and attach the plate with screws. This holds the liner in place.

D

E

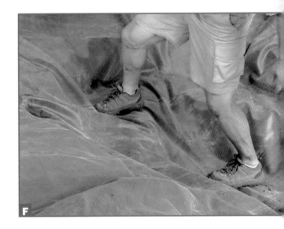
F

TIPS | DIY Network
Gardening & Landscaping

BUYING WATER PUMPS
Be sure to buy an adequate pump for the volume of water in your water feature. A common problem for new pond owners is burning out a pump that was too small for the job. Check the manufacturer's recommendations and be sure to buy enough pump for your pond.

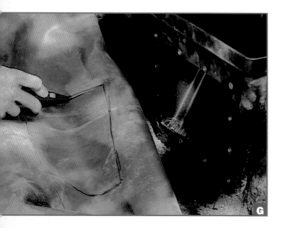

8 Use the same process to seal and attach a plate to the waterfall unit (photo I). These plates come in the water feature kit.

9 Pour stones of all sizes and shapes into the liner, and position them to hold the sides in place (photo J). Dig out additional soil beneath the edge of the liners as needed to seat larger rocks securely (photo K).

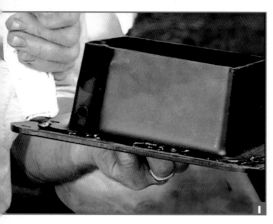

10 Set a large flat rock on the first shelf to serve as the spillway between the waterfall and the pond below (photo L). Continue to build back toward the waterfall unit with an assortment of flat and round stones to offer several different flow patterns and sounds. Plan the route of the water to the pond and place rocks to accommodate that flow. Choose rocks carefully, including a variety of flat and round rocks, both large and small (photo M).

TRANSPLANTING A FERN

In this project, Dean and Jackie uncovered a beautiful fern that they wanted to save for the garden bed around the new pond. To move a plant, first check the foliage to find the center growth of the plant. Dig deeply and on all sides of the plant, keeping as many roots and as much soil intact around it as possible. When the soil outside and beneath the root system is loosened, lift the plant from the ground. Plant it in the new location as soon as possible, and water it well. Make sure you wear gloves, long sleeves, and pants, and be careful of poison ivy. An old saying goes "Leaves of three, leave it be," referring to the characteristic three-leaf stem of poison ivy. If you do come in contact with poison ivy, be sure to wash the affected skin within 20 minutes using cold water and oil-free soap or detergent.

11 Install the pump in the skimmer according to the manufacturer's instructions (photo N). The net on the skimmer will keep large debris from reaching the pump, so the pump does not have to be cleaned routinely.

12 Add sealant between the rocks at the edges of the liner to avoid water leaking from the water feature into the yard.

13 Install the filter into the micro-falls (photo O) and turn on the water to assess the flow and check for leaks. Play with the placement of the rocks to achieve a different flow of water or different sound.

FINISHING TOUCHES

For plants to complement your new water feature, consider planting these in beds nearby: fountain grass, ostrich ferns, purple maiden grass, northern sea oats, and blue fescue "Elijah Blue."

TIPS
DIY Network
Gardening & Landscaping

MUDDY WATER
It will take the filter 2–3 days to do its work and clear up the water after you build the water feature.

CREATING A WATER GARDEN ►

Plants can grow at different depths but as you plan your pond plantings, look for vertical height as well as smaller contrasting shapes. Plant sparingly to add variety and interest to your pond, but don't overdo or you will find your pond quickly overgrown. Transplanting aquatic plants is simple, and a cost-effective way to bring new plants into your pond.

1 Many aquatic plants can be snipped and the cuttings will root in their new home, if they are not rootball-based plants (photo A). Water lettuce can simply float on the water and thrive.

2 To transplant a rootball plant, such as a cyperus papyrus, first release the root ball from the pot. This may involve cutting roots that have grown outside of the pot (photo B). Once the rootball is free of the pot, use a spade to separate the plant into sections (photo C). Transplant them to your new pond—placing them on the floor of the pond in pots to contain the roots. If you cannot transplant them immediately, protect the roots in water in the meantime.

3 During the colder months of the year, clip back the plants and take them out of the pond. Store them in a garage or other cool, dark area, and replant them in the spring.

TIPS | DIY Network
Gardening & Landscaping

KEEPING THE POND CLEAN
Check your skimmer once a week to clean out debris. During leaf season, be sure to check it more often to keep the water flowing and clean. If the skimmer is kept clean, it will keep debris from reaching the pump and causing damage.

WALLED COURTYARD

The previous owners of Kathy and Craig's home replaced the front door and porch with a picture window but left the original walkway. Visitors to the house, seeing no front door, often followed the old walkway around the house to the French doors of the master bedroom by accident. Kathy and Craig needed a plan to remove the confusing walkway and make the most of the unused side yard. Jackie Taylor and Dean Hill offered a plan to do just that.

◄ **PROJECT SUMMARY** ►

To keep deliveries and guests from ending up at the bedroom door, the walkway to the side yard of this house was removed and a stone wall courtyard put in place to visually separate the side yard from the front of the house. A stone wall planter runs along the length of the courtyard, creating a lovely view from the bedroom window, and the courtyard floor is lined with bluestone pavers and gravel. This is an advanced DIY project and will take you 1–2 weeks to complete without a crew of helpers.

BEFORE: Removing the sidewalk to the bedroom door was long overdue at this house, and the unused side yard was wasted space.

AFTER: This dramatic courtyard not only serves the practical purpose of separating the side yard from the front, but complements the style and era of the house, giving the sense that it's always been there.

◤ REMOVING A CONCRETE WALKWAY & PATIO ◥

This project involves removing two types of materials. One part is a walkway of mortared blue stone on a concrete pad. This requires cuts with a concrete saw to separate the concrete pad from the steps and walkway. The other material is patio concrete that requires a jackhammer to remove, which can be rented by the day.

You Will Need

Crowbar	Wheelbarrow
Concrete cut-off saw with diamond blade	Jackhammer
Water source and hose	Ear protection
Safety goggles and gloves	Pulverized top soil
Cold chisel	Yard compost
Mallet	Mulch (optional)
Shovels	

1 If you have stone or tile over your walkway, as this mortar bluestone, remove it with a crowbar to expose the concrete pad beneath. Make cuts into the concrete pad using a concrete cut-off saw with a diamond blade (photo A). Spray water onto the saw blade while cutting to keep it from overheating. Always wear safety goggles and gloves when breaking up concrete.

2 Use a cold chisel and mallet to pop out the cut concrete from the ground (photo B). You may need to use a jackhammer for stubborn sections of the pad (photo C).

3 Remove patio concrete by cutting through it with the cut-off saw where it joins the foundation of the house or an attached stairway.

4 Use a jackhammer to break up the freed patio slab (photo D). Be sure to wear eye and ear protection when using a jackhammer. Clear out the concrete debris with shovels (photo E). In this project, rather than hauling off the debris, the crew shoveled it into the area that would be the center of the stone wall planter, where plenty of filler would be needed under the planting soil.

5 Fill those areas cleared of concrete with soil and mulch for planting beds, if desired, or fill in with sod (photo F).

CALL BEFORE YOU DIG

Always call your local utility and cable companies to determine the path of underground utility lines before you dig in your yard.

USING A JACKHAMMER

If you are right-handed, grip the top handle of the jack hammer with your right hand, and hold the lower handle with your left hand, or the opposite if you are left handed. Apply slight constant pressure forcing the bit down, but let the machine do the work.

◄ BUILDING A COURTYARD WALL AND PLANTER ►

The courtyard includes a right-angle wall with freestanding stone corner columns and a 5-foot-wide planter running the length of the courtyard. The oversized caps for the columns are the same blue-stone pavers used for the base of the courtyard. This project requires renting a plate compactor to set the gravel base for the stone wall.

You Will Need

Tape measure	Compressed concrete blocks and caps
Landscape marking paint	Concrete block grips
String and stakes	2' or 4' level
Right angle	Mallet
Spades and shovels	Concrete adhesive
2 tons coarse base gravel	Caulk gun
Wheelbarrows	Concrete cut-off saw
Rakes	Water source and hose
Plate compactor	3 bluestone pavers
Hand tamper	Garden soil

1 Measure and mark out the border for the courtyard with landscape marking paint (photo A).

2 Outline the area for the main planter with stakes and string, measuring 5 feet wide. The planter will be supported by free-standing walls and stacked columns. Use a right angle to make sure the string layout for the planter has perfectly square corners (photo B).

TIPS | DIY Network
Gardening & Landscaping

CONCRETE BLOCK

Consult your concrete block manufacturer to determine the quantities and types of block you need. This project used regular wall stone, column stone, and freestanding wall stone that were secured with pins from the manufacturer.

3 Excavate the area for the base of the courtyard walls—10 inches deep and 10 inches wide (photo C). Dig out the soil from the outlined area, depositing the excess in the middle area where the planter will be located inside the wall (photo D).

4 Fill the area excavated for the wall with gravel (photo E). Smooth the gravel out with rakes and then tamp it down using a plate com-pactor (photo F). Tamp down any remaining loose stone with a hand tamp to ensure a flat gravel platform for the wall (photo G).

5 Lay down the base course of block for the perimeter of the wall and the planter. Check each block for level as you go, set it in place with a mallet (photo H), and check for level again (photo I). Having the base course perfectly level is critical for an even wall.

6 Use half-blocks to create 20x20-inch corner columns that the 12-inch wall will "die into." Check each block for level as you build the columns as well.

7 When the base course is laid (photo J), fill in the sides of the trench with dirt, being sure to work soil down to the bottom of the trench with a shovel (photo K).

TIPS | DIY Network Gardening & Landscaping

USING BLOCK GRIPS
Use block grips inserted in holes in the top of the blocks to make it easier to lift these nearly 85-pound weights.

8 Lay the second course of block on top of the first and secure the blocks (photo L). The product used in this project was secured with pins provided by the manufacturer.

9 Use a generous bead of concrete adhesive between the courses of block for the stone columns (photo M). Be sure to turn the column blocks as you build so that the exposed sides are the same texture as those of the wall block.

10 Build the additional courses of the wall, using the concrete cut-off saw to cut blocks as necessary to fit the wall. Be sure to stagger the block seams with each course of the wall. Build the wall with four courses of block. Then set block caps in place as the final course, securing them with concrete adhesive (photo N).

11 Build up five courses of block for the columns. Apply concrete adhesive to the top course and set bluestone pavers in place as caps (photo O). Measure the overhang on each side of the column and move the cap so it is even on all sides (photo P). Press down on the column cap to help it adhere.

12 Rake the excavated soil evenly inside the wall planter. Add a mixture of half pulverized top soil and half composted yard waste for garden soil to a depth of at least 12 inches.

◣ BUILDING THE COURTYARD ◣

This courtyard is a formal style using rectangles on a grid. An informal style would use curvalinear and flowing lines instead. The courtyard inside the wall includes ground-level garden beds, a floor of bluestone pavers, and pea gravel.

You Will Need

Shovel	Pennsylvania bluestone pavers
Rakes	2' or 4' level
Landscape marking paint	Pea gravel
Tape measure	Push broom
Metal edging with spikes	Garden soil
Mallet	Plants and shrubs for planting
Metal hack saw or reciprocating saw	Mulch

1 Mark out the areas of the courtyard for planting beds with landscape marking paint (photo A).

2 Install metal edging along the markings to define the area for the beds (photo B). Be sure to situate the edging so that the slots for the stakes face the inside of the bed. Use a mallet to secure it in place (photo C). Cut the last length of edging to size with a hack saw saw, if needed.

TIPS | DIY Network Gardening & Landscaping

LEVELING PAVERS

Be sure to always level pavers before walking on them. They crack easily when they aren't balanced.

CREATING CORNERS WITH METAL EDGING

If you don't have a corner piece to make a clean right angle with metal edging, make a cut into the edging at the point you need a right angle. Only cut halfway through its height (photo, below, top). Then, bend the edging on the cut-line, folding it onto itself to make a good crease (photo below, bottom). Open it back up to 90 degrees and secure it in place with stakes.

3 Level the ground in the courtyard for each paver before placing it. Then measure and set pavers 6 inches apart (photo D). Check each stone for level as you go, brushing away or filling in dirt as necessary to support the paver evenly. Once in place, test the pavers for any instability by walking on them (photo E).

4 Fill in around the pavers with pea gravel. Haul the gravel in wheelbarrows and deposit it between pavers with a shovel, using rakes and brooms to sweep the gravel into place (photo F).

5 Fill the garden beds with soil, install plantings, add a layer of mulch (photo G), and water the new plantings well.

FINISHING TOUCHES

Plant a mixture of flowering plants, shrubs, and decorative grasses in your courtyard, using the center of the courtyard for a focal point such as the birdbath planter with vining and flowering plants installed in this project. For a more private area, plant a screen of evergreens on the edge.

BACKYARD BOARDWALK

Lila and Foster built their waterfront home in Charleston, South Carolina, themselves. However, they ran out of ideas when it came to getting from the house to the water. *Grounds for Improvement* Landscape Designer Dean Hill devised a plan to open up the possibilities of this backyard.

◀ **PROJECT SUMMARY** ▶

Jackie Taylor and Dean Hill helped these homeowners and their friends build a curved boardwalk from their house to the marsh, and built custom-designed lawn chairs for a seating area to enjoy the view.

BEFORE: These homeowners had a dock out on the water, but just a bare lawn between the house and the dock.

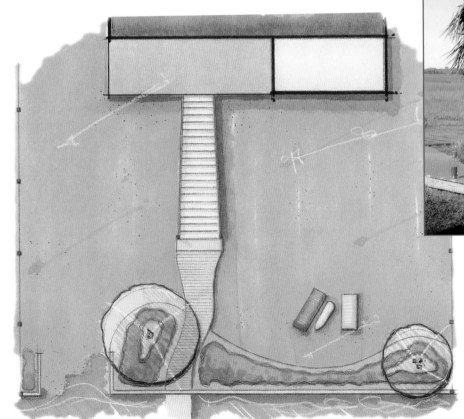

AFTER: A new curvalinear boardwalk makes going out to the water more inviting-- especially with the colorful new seating area for taking in the sun or watching birds on the water.

◀ CONSTRUCTING THE BOARDWALK ▶

This boardwalk design involves a wide landing that tapers into a 3-foot-wide walkway to the water. Use 4x4s and 2x6s to frame the walkway, and 12-foot composite 2x6 planks for the boardwalk surface. Use a garden hose as a handy tool to help visualize the curvilinear edge of the walkway before cutting the boards. A pneumatic nail gun and screw gun will simplify this job immensely.

You Will Need

Landscape marking paint	String
Circular saw	(32) 12' composite planks
(8) 4"x4"x8' composite lumber	(15) 2"x6"x12' composite lumber
Safety goggles and gloves	#10 box of 3" galvanized screws
Posthole digger or auger	Chalk
Tape measure and pencil	Miter saw
4' level	Pneumatic nail gun
Quick-set concrete	Screw gun
2 stakes	Garden hose

1 Mark out the area for your new walkway using landscape paint. Specifically mark the midpoint where the center joist will go, and mark the depth of the landing as well. In this case, the project extended an existing landing out 18 inches.

2 Wearing safety goggles and gloves, use a circular saw to cut the composite 4x4s into 18-inch posts for the framing. Cut slowly through pressure-treated lumber so the saw doesn't bind or grab. Keep the post flush against the fence of the saw at all times for a straight cut.

3 Use a posthole diggger to dig holes for the corner posts of the landing (photo A) and put the posts in place. The far side of the post should measure exactly 18 inches from the existing walkway or stairs for the landing extension.

4 Check the posts for plumb and level, and use quick-set concrete to set them in place. Be sure the posts are set 1 inch lower than the existing stairway landing so when the decking boards are attached, the new walkway will be flush with the landing.

5 Pound two temporary stakes 18 inches out from the existing stairway landing, on the outside of the installed corner posts. Run a string between them at the height of the corner posts (photo B). This will establish the height for the additional post tops. Any point along the string should be exactly 18 inches from the edge of the landing (photo C). Install additional posts along the string line, between the corner posts.

6 Attach framing boards, called stringers, to the outside of the support posts, flush with the top. Check each stringer for level and secure it with 3-inch galvanized screws.

7 Install additional support posts at the point the walkway will taper to a 3-foot width. Check the posts for level (photo D). Set the stringer on the back corner of the supporting post and mark the angle of the square post onto the stringer. Make the bevel cut of the angle with a miter saw. Secure the angled board to the post.

8 As you build out the frame, fill the inside with joists to support the walkway. Use a pneumatic nail gun to nail the joists into place (photo E).

9 Next, secure the decking boards with a screw gun. These composite boards are easy to work with—they have no splinters, take no maintenance, and won't fade. Use a nail to create a uniform, ⅛" gap between the boards (photo F). Both ends of the board will overhang the frame. The sides will be marked and cut to shape later.

D

E

F

10 When the decking is installed, use a garden hose as a guide to help visualize the radius down the pathway (photo G). Position the hose making sure that the line falls outside the framing underneath. Scribe the line of the hose onto the decking boards with chalk.

11 Use a circular saw to cut along the marked curve (photo H). Then, measure from the cut side to mark a mirror-image curve on the other side of the walkway. Cut that side as well to finish the smooth curves of the walkway.

BUILDING CUSTOM LAWN CHAIRS

The frame for these chairs is made of a double thickness of pressure-treated plywood and the slats are cut from composite 2x6s.

You Will Need

- (9) 4' x 8' sheets of pressure-treated plywood
- (14) 2" x 6" x 8' pressure-treated pine
- Safety goggles and gloves
- Cordless jigsaw
- Circular saw
- 2x4 pressure-treated boards
- Exterior-grade screws
- Drill and screwdriver bits
- Power sander and sandpaper
- 1 gallon primer
- 1 gallon exterior-grade latex paint, blue
- 1 gallon exterior-grade latex paint, saffron
- Power sprayer or paintbrushes

1 Mark the outline for the chairs onto pressure-treated plywood (see page 172 for pattern), drawing four cutouts per chair since each side of a chair is made of a double thickness of plywood.

2 Wearing safety goggles and gloves, use a cordless jigsaw to cut carefully along the outlined area (photo A, next page). Use a circular saw to cut 2x6s into 24-inch slats for the chair seats and backs. Mark and cut pressure-treated 2x4s into braces for the backs of the chairs.

TIPS
DIY Network
Gardening & Landscaping

MAKE EVEN SLATS
Use a small wooden spacer between the slats of the chair to ensure uniformity as you attach them.

3 Assemble double thicknesses of the plywood cutouts for the furniture sides: Align the ends and fasten them together at the corners with exterior-grade screws (photo B). Then, use a power sander to smooth the edges thoroughly to make sure there are no splinters. Use safety goggles while assembling the sides and sanding.

4 Secure treated braces at the back of the chair between the sides for strength, drilling screws through the sides of the chair into the braces.

5 Attach 2x6 slats with decking screws for the seating surface. Allow a uniform, 1-inch overhang (photo C).

6 Prime the chairs, and then paint them with exterior-grade latex paint (photo D). Use two coats of paint whenever painting exterior wood. Then—after they dry—sit back and relax!

FINISHING TOUCHES

Create planting beds along the walkway or around the seating area with plants, shrubs, and grasses native to your region. In this project, the crew brought a marsh effect into the yard by planting pink muhly grass and shenandoah switch grass in pulverized topsoil, topping it off with pine straw. Dean also used an old wooden surf board of Foster's as a tabletop, mounting it on legs and installing it into the ground between the chairs.

WROUGHT-IRON RENOVATION

This homeowner, Kelly, discovered an old wrought-iron fence at an antique show. She knew it would be a great addition to her 1930's stone home, she just didn't know where. So Jackie Taylor and Dean Hill from *Grounds for Improvement* stepped in to install her salvaged fence with style and give her ho-hum house and garden a splash of color.

◀ **PROJECT SUMMARY** ▶

The homeowner and the *Grounds for Improvement* team custom-trimmed some pressure-treated 4x4s to anchor the fence and redesigned and expanded her front flowerbeds. They also brightened up the house itself with accent paint on the shutters and front door.

BEFORE: Although the front walkway benefited from a nice planting bed, nothing else supplied color or character to the home's curb appeal.

AFTER: Kelly and the *Grounds for Improvement* team installed an appealing antique wrought-iron fence around the front walkway, cleaned up the garden space, and added some color to the predominantly white house by painting the front door and shutters.

◀ **BUILDING A SALVAGED WROUGHT-IRON FENCE** ▶

This fence could not be rebuilt as it was originally, so each section of wrought iron was instead fitted between wooden posts, which were covered with fluted trim. Each piece of antique wrought iron is unique, not exact in size or pattern, so checking visually for level is all that's needed in putting in this fence.

You Will Need

Wrought-iron fence panels	Paintbrushes
Reciprocating saw	Brad nailer and nails
Tape measure and pencil	Drill and bits
(8) 4x4 pressure-treated posts	Landscape marking paint
Circular saw	Auger
(16) 1" x 4" x 8' pressure-treated trim, fluted	Lug bolts
(16) 1" x 6" x 8' pressure-treated trim, plain	Socket wrench
	4' level
(8) 6x6 post caps	Quick-set concrete
Paint primer	Water source
Exterior-grade paint	Scrap rebar or stake

1 Lay out the wrought iron panels to determine placement for the fence and how many posts you will need (photo A). Some scrolling on this fence was removed with a reciprocating saw to expose more of the peg on the end of the fence to recess securely into the post.

2 Measure the height for the wood posts to support the wrought iron, and mark the posts for cutting. In this project, the pressure treated 4x4s were cut to 78" (48" to be trimmed and 30" to be set into the ground). Use a circular saw to cut the posts to size. Also, cut the trim to length (photo B).

3 Seal the trim and post caps with primer. Add two coats of paint. Allow each coat of primer or paint to dry completely before applying the next coat. Paint is dry when it is no longer tacky to the touch.

4 Use fluted 1x4 trim for front and back sides of the posts that will be most visible; use plain 1x4 trim on the sides of the post that will attach to the iron fencing. Wrap the posts with trim, secure it using a brad nailer (photo C) and leave 30 inches of the pressure-treated post exposed to set into the ground.

5 Measure the height of the bars (pegs) that protrude from the side of the wrought iron fence and transfer those measurements to the wood posts for drilling. Drill holes through the posts with a paddle bit where the wrought iron will attach (photo D). Attach the post caps with a brad nailer.

6 Measure the locations for the first two posts and mark them with landscape paint. Use an auger to dig holes 30 inches deep for the posts (photo E). Antique wrought-iron panels may not be equal sizes, so dig one hole at a time using each fence piece to set the position of the next post.

7 If the ends of your fence are flat, without pegs, as in this project, drill three holes into the metal in the same positions as the pegs on the other side. This side will be secured to the post with bolts.

C

D

TIPS | DIY Network
Gardening & Landscaping

ESTATE SALES

If you want to consider adding some character—like a wrought-iron fence—to your yard, do what Kelly did and go to an estate sale. Estate sales often include fixtures like doors, windows, and fencing, as well as many antiques.

E

8 Set in the first post (photo F) and fill around it with soil temporarily. After the wrought iron panels are in place, the posts will be secured more permanently with cement. Measure out the distance for the second posthole. Dig the hole, and set the post in the same manner.

9 Fit the first panel of wrought iron into position (photo G). The horizontal bars (pegs) protruding from one end of the panel fit into the holes drilled on the second post. Secure the other end of this panel to the first post with a bolt through the holes drilled in the flat side of the fence in step 7 (photo H). Use the next panel to determine placement of the next posthole. Continue in the same manner with each section of fence.

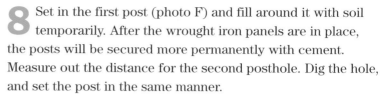

TIPS DIY Network
Gardening & Landscaping

FOLLOW THE SLOPE OF THE YARD
When putting in a fence, follow the slope of the yard rather than trying to make all of the posts level across the top.

10 Check the first post for plumb and set it with quick-set concrete mix and water (photo I). Use a scrap of rebar, or other stake, to make sure the water goes to the bottom of the hole and to press out any air bubbles near the post. Let the concrete in the first hole dry completely (several hours) before setting the second post to ensure a tight fit. Continue until all posts are set.

FINISHING TOUCHES

Add plants, such as day lilies, behind the fence to soften the walkway. Create a free-flowing garden in front of the fence to give more visual impact and highlight the fence. Add mulch to both garden areas. You may also want to do as this crew did and give the house a facelift with new paint on the front door and window shutters.

TRANSPLANTING MATURE SHRUBS

Dean Hill says that plants are like furniture and sometimes it's time to change the layout of the room! He showed this home-owner how to move a mature Nandina bush.

1 A great time to transplant is in the spring—the ground is moist and the air is cool and damp, so the plant won't dehydrate.

2 Tie up the limbs of larger plants to allow access to the roots.

3 Work a sharp spade around the rootball of the plant, taking as much existing soil and root as possible.

4 After transplanting, prune the plant. The less growth or foliage it has, the less require-ment for feeding and moisture while it is going through the shock of transplanting.

STONE TERRACING

Jane and Craig have a big family and wanted a backyard to entertain and accommodate lots of people. Unfortunately, right out their back door the yard sloped down a steep grade with little room for even a grill. Nothing would grow on the hill, and Craig was concerned about the bank eroding. With a crew of friends and the help of *Grounds for Improvement's* Dean Hill and Jackie Taylor, this backyard was transformed into a beautiful terraced landscape.

◣ PROJECT SUMMARY ◢

This backyard was once a precarious place for anyone stepping out of Jane and Craig's back door. Now a natural stone stairway and terraced planting beds connect the lower yard to the house for the first time. Landscape Designer Dean Hill, with the help of Jackie Taylor, showed this family how to build a stone slab stairway into the hill, create a boulder foundation for a landing or terrace, and build a retaining wall with a patio on top for grilling out and entertaining friends.

BEFORE: A too-steep sloping backyard prevented this family from having easy access to the woods and creek below and left few options for entertaining guests outdoors.

AFTER: Beautiful planting beds terraced on the side of the hill with a natural stone slab stairway have transformed this yard from useless to priceless.

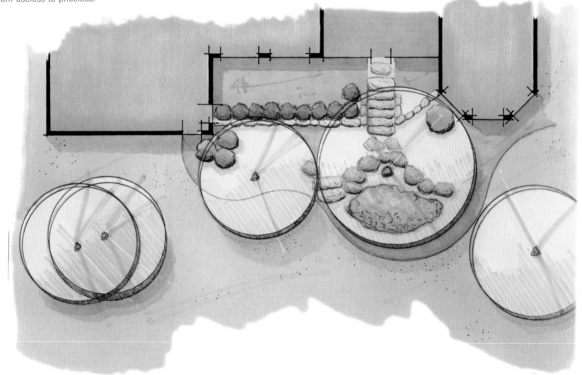

◣ CREATING A STONE-SLAB STAIRWAY ◢

You will need to rent a compact utility loader for this project to move the heavy stones and slabs. While this project requires a lot of brawn because of the heavy slabs, the results will be long-lasting and well worth it. The stairway is built with a 14-inch tread on the steps and a 3-foot landing at the door.

You Will Need

String level	Compact utility loader
Tape measure	(6) 3' x 4' x6" snapped steps
Landscape marking paint	Landscape bar
Shovels	4' level
Hand tamp	

1 Determine the rise (height) and run (width) of the steps according to your embankment. To do this, hold a string level at the foundation of the house and extend it to the point the stairway will begin. Holding it in level position, measure its height at the bottom stair (photo A). This measurement is the rise—the change in elevation from the existing slope to the future height. Mark the location for the stairway with landscape paint, including the location of the back of the top step and the front of the bottom step.

2 Building the stairway from the bottom up, use shovels to excavate the area for the bottom step first, making sure to dig out sufficient area for the width and depth of the step. Use a hand tamp to flatten the surface before putting the step in place (photo B).

3 Using the compact utility loader, place the first step in the area excavated (photo C). Then, manually work one end of the heavy slab at a time, maneuvering it into place. Be sure to have sufficient crew to move the slab without causing injury.

4 Check visually for center and placement, and use a landscape bar and shovels to make final adjustments. Check the step for level left to right, and make sure it has a slight fall away from the house for drainage from back to front.

SURE FOOTING

With natural stone steps, you may want to increase the tread, or depth, of the stairs to offer sure footing and comfort—people often are not used to going down steep natural steps.

5 Dig out the soil to make space for the next stair, backfilling behind the previous stair and tamping the surface down after excavating, making sure it is even. To position the second step, set it on top of the first step and maneuver it back into place for the appropriate tread—in this case, 14 inches. Check the step for level and backfill behind it (photo D).

6 Repeat the process for each subsequent stair (photo E), making sure to create a 14-inch tread, and checking each stair for level before moving to the next.

7 To create a flat landing from a slope at the bottom of the stairs, see the next project, "Building a Boulder Foundation."

FOUNDATION FOR FLAGSTONES

Flagstones need a very flat foundation under them to avoid breaking, so make sure to level the area completely before laying in flagstone. On the other hand, if your flagstones are too large, they can easily be broken into smaller pieces to fit your landscaping needs.

◄ BUILDING A BOULDER FOUNDATION FOR A LANDING OR TERRACE ►

This project creates a flat landing area at the bottom of the stone stairway using boulders. A large flagstone tops this newly leveled landing for a hard surface that continues the natural stone theme and lends added color and texture. You'll need an easy way to move heavy boulders for this project—a ball cart will be invaluable. It's a wide, wheeled dolly with rounded sides used to move heavy objects like boulders and rootballs.

You Will Need

Landscape marking paint	Hand tamp
Shovels and spades	Flagstone
Boulders	Mulch
Ball cart	Native foliage and grasses

1 Mark out the dimensions of the area to build up with boulders. Dig out the foundation for the boulders at the bottom of the area (photo A). Be sure to dig deeply enough into the hillside—boulders need their entire base supported. Use a ball cart to move the boulders to the work area (photo B).

2 Stack the boulders together, allowing some pockets between them to fill later with plantings (photo C). This will give the foundation for the landing a more natural look.

3 When the boulders are in place, backfill and level the soil over them. Tamp the area well to ensure it is as flat as possible. Lay down a large flagstone for a solid stepping surface on the landing.

4 Fill the planting pockets between the boulders with mulch and native foliage and grasses.

◢ BUILDING A RETAINING WALL ◣

This natural stone retaining wall will not only keep your bank from eroding, it can also provide a terrace on top for plantings or a location for grilling. The wall is built with five courses—6 tons—of wall stone. Rent a compact utility loader to move this heavy stone.

You Will Need

Landscape marking paint	Rock hammer
Shovels	Sledge hammer
6 tons of white-to-gray wall stone	Hand tamp
Compact utility loader	2 tons of drain gravel
Tape measure	Mulch
Safety glasses and gloves	Flagstones
Cold chisel	New plants

1 Mark out the location of the retaining wall with landscape paint. The first course—or row—of stone at the base of the wall will be submerged to half the height of the stair next to it, which is the second stair from the bottom of the stairway (photo A).

2 Dig out the foundation for the first course of stone. Lay the stones in place, spacing them as closely together as possible, flipping the stone, repositioning it with soil beneath, or breaking off portions of it as necessary to achieve visual level across the top of the course (photo B). Use a cold chisel, rock hammer, or sledge hammer, as appropriate, to break the stone. Always use safety goggles and gloves for this kind of work.

SETTING A FIRM FOUNDATION

When laying stone, look first for height—that the stones are level left to right and with each other. Then look closely at the edges of the stones that will rest against each other and the relationship between them; lay them as closely together as possible and with as minimal joint as possible. This may involve testing several different placements of the rocks against each other to find the best fit. Make sure you periodically step back from the course you are laying to see whether it is visually level and the joints appear as tight as possible from a few steps away.

TOOLS FOR WORKING WITH ROCK

Three tools offer different methods to make working with rock more manageable. The first is a cold chisel, a tool with a blunt end, which is used with a sledge hammer to score the edge of a rock where you want to break it. Another is a rock hammer. The flat side can chip off bumps and fragments, or texture the rock as you need it. The third is a sledge hammer to break large rocks into smaller pieces. To break off a portion of a large rock, set it on another rock with the excess hanging off, unsupported. Use a sledge hammer to strike the very edge of the rock repeatedly until it breaks along the support underneath.

3 Place the second course, staggering the joints at least 4 inches from the first course. Continue setting stones in the same manner for this course, breaking stones as necessary to fit and to keep the joints staggered (photo C). Once the second course is complete, use gravel to backfill 6 inches behind the wall (photo D), and soil to fill in the rest. Repeat the same building process for each course to the top of the stairs, backfilling as you go.

TIPS | DIY Network Gardening & Landscaping

BACKFILLING OPTIONS

To backfill a low retaining wall, you can simply use the soil you've dug out for the wall because water will still drain through it. You can also use stone to backfill the first 6 inches behind the wall to aid drainage. The need may depend on the height of the wall—if you build a tall wall of natural stone, be sure to backfill with drainage stone so that hydrostatic pressure does not build up behind the wall.

4 After the top course is laid, backfill the wall and cover the ground at the top of the wall with mulch. Rake the area around the top of the wall level to create a terrace for grilling or planting. For a grill, make sure the ground is as flat as possible, and lay a large flagstone down to hold the grill. Place another flagstone a step away for a solid area to stand while grilling. Add mulch between the flagstones and install plantings to complete the new landscape (photo E).

5 Build a landing at the top of the stairs using rock from the retaining wall as a border and filling it with gravel.

D

E

FINISHING TOUCHES

Use additional stair slabs to break the slope leading down the hill. Build smaller boulder terraces with planting beds across the face of the hill for plants such as hosta, ferns, hydrangea, and shrubs such as boxwood.

3

Backyard Decking

A deck is a great outdoor space that quickly becomes indispensable. It's practical for eating or sunning, and doesn't have to look like a dock without a lake! This chapter offers three directions to take your decking—and those are just a sampling of the options available. From an enduring cedar deck and elegant gazebo to a pet-friendly, low-maintenance composite deck, or a two-tiered, sophisticated paver-patio deck, choose your look and your materials based on your outdoor lifestyle. These projects will take plenty of brawn, so be sure you have a good crew to make it happen and tools enough for everyone.

WEDDING GAZEBO

John and Sharon offered to host their son's wedding ceremony in their yard, only to realize they were not prepared. The yard needed a lot of work and lacked an attractive focal point.

■ PROJECT SUMMARY ■

Dean Hill and Jackie Taylor, along with the homeowners' friends and family, built a deck, assembled a gazebo, and made some creative lighting to get the yard ready for the big day. The completed gazebo is a beautiful addition to any lawn and a lovely backdrop for an intimate backyard wedding or other celebration.

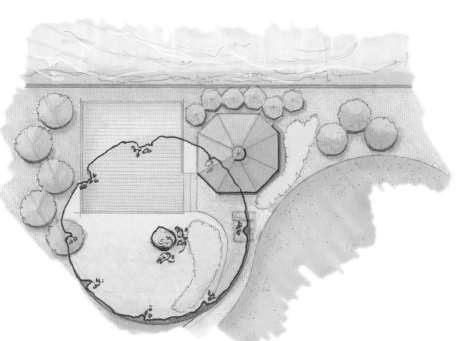

BEFORE: These homeowners had a lovely backyard on a creek with a lot of potential to develop before hosting their son's wedding.

AFTER: A beautiful new creek-side deck and gazebo give the backyard intimate charm and a focal point for the wedding ceremony.

◄ BUILDING A CEDAR DECK ►

Cedar is a fragrant wood that takes on deep rich tones when it is wet. It is also naturally weather and insect resistant. This deck is 10 square feet made with cedar supports and cedar decking. Rent a compact utility loader with an auger head for this project.

You Will Need

Landscape marking paint	Tape measure and pencil
Shovels	String
Rakes	(30) 2" x 6" x 12' cedar planks
Wheelbarrow	Circular saw
Compact utility loader with auger head	Safety goggles and gloves
Posthole digger	Drill and bits
(5) 4" x 4" x 8' pressure-treated posts	lug bolts
10 bags quick-set concrete mix	3" galvanized or coated decking screws
4' level	Reciprocating saw
Water source and hose	(20) 2" x 10" x 12' cedar planks
Scrap rebar or stake	(3) 3' x 4' x 6" snapped steps

1 Use landscape marking paint to mark the location for the deck posts (photo A). Then use shovels, rakes, and wheelbarrows to clear out any shrubs, stones, or loose debris from the deck area.

2 Next, dig the postholes. Use a compact utility loader with an auger head to dig 30 inches into the ground for the posts (photo B). Use a posthole digger to clean out the holes.

3 Place the first pressure-treated post into the ground (photo C) and fill the hole around it with quick-set concrete mix. Add water, working it to the bottom of the hole with a stake or length of rebar. Check the post for level and plumb.

4 Put the next post in place, making sure the distance measures 10 feet from the outside of one post to the outside of the other. Use a string to make sure the second post is in line with the first (photo D). Set the second post with concrete mix in the same manner as for step 3.

5 Connect the posts with 2x10 cedar planks (photo E). To do this, mark the planks for cutting and cut to size using a circular saw. Make sure to wear safety goggles and gloves whenever using the circular saw. Secure the planks to the outside of the posts with lug bolts (photo F), checking for level with each board. The excess height of the posts will be cut off later.

6 Level the ground inside the frame with a shovel, then use additional 2x6 cedar planks on the inside of the frame as joists. Secure the joists to the frame with decking screws (photo G). Make sure to support the deck's framing with enough joists in the center.

7 Next, install a center support post: Dig an additional post hole 30 inches deep in the center of the frame, next to a joist (photo H). Place the center post in the hole, holding the post flush against a joist. Check for plumb and level. Set the post as the others in step 3. Bolt the joist to the post for added strength.

8 Use a reciprocating saw to cut the support posts flush to the frame (photo I). Be sure this cut is completely level.

9 Next, take measurements between the joists for cross supports. Mark the measurements on 2x10 planks and make the cuts with a circular saw. Fit them between the joists and secure them into place with decking screws (photo J).

TIPS | DIY Network
Gardening & Landscaping

PREVENT WARPING

To minimize warping with deck planks, look at the grain of the wood on the end of the plank and see the half-circle or "cup" of the grain. Lay the board "cup down" when you secure it.

10 Then, secure the decking. Lay out 2x10 cedar planks on the frame, leaving a 2-inch overhang. Use screws as spacers between the boards to keep them even, and secure each board to each joist with decking screws (photo K).

11 On an uneven edge of the decking, mark the 2-inch over-hang with a chalk line. Use a circular saw to cut along the chalk line for an even edge (photo L). (If you are joining two decks, as was done in this project, see the sidebar on the following page before completing this step.)

TIPS | DIY Network
Gardening & Landscaping

CENTER SUPPORT

This deck uses five support posts instead of four. With four posts, the center of the floor might have flux or sponginess. A center post will add the needed support for a solid floor.

Buying a gazebo kit makes construction a breeze—you just fit the tongue-and-groove boards together and secure with screws according to the manufacturer's instructions. Many gazebo styles also come with their own flooring.

You Will Need

12'x12' gazebo kit	Drill and bits
Screws	

1 Begin with two of the gazebo wall panels. Fit the tongue and groove together (photo A), and secure them with screws through the pre-drilled holes (photo B). Work around the octagon, securing one panel at a time. Attach the door by sliding the tongue-and-groove posts together and screwing the door into place as well.

2 Mark the center point of the back of the deck. Move the gazebo into final position, placing the center of the back of the gazebo on the center point marked (photo C). Drive screws through the wall material into the floor at an angle. Then pre-drill holes in the bottom frame of the gazebo, and secure it to the floor boards with screws as well.

In this project, Dean's design included joining the new deck to the lower stair of an existing deck (photo below, top). To do this, before laying the new boards that will meet the old deck, measure and cut the angles for the boards. Lay one plank in place on the new deck, overlapping the old deck stair, draw a line along the edge of the stair on the underside of the new cedar plank. This is the cut line for the board. Repeat this with each board that will join the existing deck; then cut the angles with a miter saw. Install the angled planks onto the new deck, flush with the old stairway (photo below, bottom). Then, proceed to trim the edge of the deck to a 2-inch overhang, as on page 117 step 11.

3 Assemble the roof joists for the gazebo separately, attaching them to the central cylinder with screws drilled at an angle through the pre-drilled holes (photo D). Raise the roof assembly into position on the gazebo. Notches in the rafters allow the joists to fit snugly on top of the wall panels (photo E). Secure the rafters to the gazebo with 3-inch screws.

4 Install the fascia boards into slots along the rafters to support the roof panels (photo F). Then, install the roof panels. Make sure the edge of each panel is lined up with the center of the rafter on which it rests (photo G). Screw it into place. Then, install cedar shingles over the seams where the roof panels meet (photo H). Top the roof with the finial provided with the kit.

5 Finally, add steps to connect the yard to the gazebo.

CREATING CANDLE FLOWER POTS

Wax in bead form makes candle-making a cinch. You can buy it at any craft store. Many stores sell beads in a variety of colors and fragrances, as well. And, the beads are so easy to work with even children can make these candles.

You Will Need

Terra-cotta pots	Sand
Floral adhesive	Wax beads
Reindeer moss	Wicks

1 Use floral adhesive to glue moss onto the rims and sides of the terra-cotta pots in random patterns (photo A). Be sure to wear gloves when using floral adhesive.

2 Fill the pots with sand, stopping an inch from the top and place a wick in the center of the pot.

3 Then, fill the rest of the pot with wax beads (photo B). Cut the wick to a half inch above the wax beads. When done, Place the pots in groups around the yard and in the gazebo (photo C).

FINISHING TOUCHES

Set lush plants, such as ferns, in eye-catching planters around the gazebo interspersed with crafted candle pots. In this project, reindeer moss was used to decorate the pots to create a natural look. Add decorative ribbons and bows to the gazebo, and use simple white chairs for the guests. Place ribbons on the backs of the chairs that are on the sides of the aisle. Accent the gazebo with silky, flowing materials that will add movement to the landscape with the breeze.

MULTI-LEVEL PAVER DECK

Bob and Nancy are devoted to maintaining their attractive yard, but almost a third of it is taken up by an unsightly, elevated deck and a seldom-used, above-ground pool. So following Dean Hill's design Jackie Taylor, the homeowners, and some of their friends and family, go to work on a complete overhaul of the area, creating a new, relaxing space for entertaining.

◢ PROJECT SUMMARY ◣

This backyard overhaul involved removing a deck swimming pool, demolishing the old wooden deck, and replacing it with a two-level, paver deck complete with a copper counter, a few new trees for privacy, and a planter to complement the deck.

BEFORE: The raised deck and outdoor pool were such an eyesore to these homeowners that they rarely ventured into their own backyard.

AFTER: Now, a stunning new deck offers a tranquil and private place to sun or a grand space for entertaining guests.

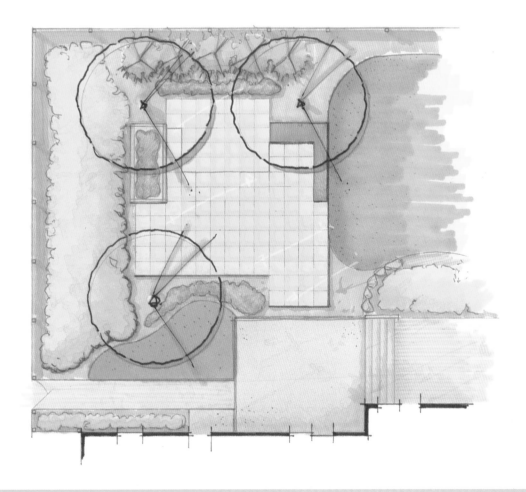

DECK DEMOLITION

Most of the demolition work on a deck is done with a sledge hammer, though a pry bar will also come in handy. In this project, the decking and floor joists were removed, but the support posts were kept in place for the new deck.

You Will Need

Safety goggles and gloves	Pry bars
Sledge hammers	Reciprocating saw

1 Wearing safety goggles and gloves, remove the railings and decking. Use a sledge hammer to strike the overhang of the deck boards from below to force the boards off of the frame (photo A). Watch out for flying nails and splinters of wood.

2 Continue hitting the board from underneath, separating it from the joists. Use a pry bar as needed to release a board from a stubborn nail or screw (photo B).

3 Carry the boards with the nails facing down for safety as you clear them away (photo C). You may want to save some of the boards to reuse in other projects, such as the copper counter-top in this section.

4 When the decking is demolished, remove the joists as well. Leave the support posts in place to use for the framing of the new deck. Cut off any unneeded support posts at ground level with a reciprocating saw.

◄ **BUILDING A MULTI-LEVEL PAVER DECK** ►

This deck is built on the site of the previous deck, using the original support posts, which are still in place. The deck is laid with attractive stone pavers rather than wood; the joists are spaced 2 feet apart on the frame, and additional support posts are added to the middle of the deck for strength. The pavers are 88 pounds each so be sure you have plenty of help and muscle for this project.

You Will Need

Speed square and pencil	Quick-set concrete
Tape measure	Scrap 2x2 or rebar for mixing
Salvaged decking materials	Self-adhesive, waterproof joist membrane
Reciprocating saw	Utility knife
Safety goggles and gloves	(100) 24x24 deckstone pavers
2' or 4' level	(160) 24x24 sonorastone pavers
4" x 6" pressure-treated lumber, 8'-14' lengths	(100) paver brackets with bolts, washers, and screws
(1) 15 lb box 2½-3" deck screws	Posthole digger
Drill and bits	Hammer and nails
(60) 4x6 joist hangers	Sand (if needed)
Circular saw	Copper sheeting
(4) 4" x 4" x 8' pressure-treated posts	Tin snips or electric metal shears

1 Cut the existing support posts to height. To do this, mark the first post using a speed square and a pencil (photo A) about 3 inches above the ground. Then, make the cut with a reciprocating saw (photo B).

2 To mark the second post for cutting, lay a plank on top of the first cut post and, placing a level on top of the plank, lift the board until it is level (photo C). Then, mark the second post at the bottom edge of the level board. Transfer the marks to each side of the post with a speed square, and cut the post. Repeat this process for each support post so the deck framing will be level, not slope with any grade of the ground.

3 Attach 4x6 timbers along the top of the posts to create the deck frame and check for level. Drive decking screws through the 4x6 into the post at an angle (photo D).

4 Pre-drill recessed holes into the framing with a paddle bit (photo E) and install lag bolts and washers to give the beams a tight grip (photo F).

5 Measure and mark 2-foot increments with a pencil along the deck frame. Then, position 4x6 joist hangers on the frame, centering each on a mark. The joists will sit inside the hangers and support the deck pavers. Hold the hanger flush with the bottom of the frame (photo G), and secure it to the frame with screws, making sure the opening of the hanger is 3½ inches wide when installed.

6 To support the weight of the pavers—a hefty 22 pounds per square foot—install a support beam down the center of the deck as well (photo H). This creates two boxes, or frames, to support the decking.

7 Install the joists: First, mark and cut the boards to length with a circular saw. Then, insert the boards into the joist hangers (photo I). Some of the hangers may need adjusting to ensure the joist is flush and level with the cross beam (photo J).

TIPS | DIY Network Gardening & Landscaping

RECESSED BOLTS
Use a paddle bit to predrill holes for lag bolts so the head can be flush with the wood.

8 For extra support at the center of each half of the deck (from the center support beam to the frame), use a post-hole digger to dig a posthole and install a center post with quick-setting concrete and water (see page 101 for more information on setting posts). Cut the post to size as in step 2. Then secure the post to the joist with nails.

9 Next, protect the joists from water damage with a waterproof membrane. Simply roll out this self-adhesive material over the joist, cut it to length, peel off the paper backing, and press it to the joist. Extend the membrane onto the framing so that the end of the joist is protected too (photo K). Press the overhang of the membrane to the sides of the joists. Where the membrane spans a right angle, at the point the joists meet the framing, cut the membrane with a utility knife at a 45-degree angle (photo L) and press each flap down to the side of the joist and the frame.

10 Lay the pavers in a "soldier course" of one color around the perimeter; a "field" of another color or pattern will be laid inside the perimeter later. Make sure each paver overlaps only half of each joist (photo M).

11 Secure the outer pavers on the perimeter with bolts. To do this, attach a bracket to the predrilled hole on the underside of the paver (photo N). Lay the paver in place and reach underneath to mark the position of the bracket against the framing timber. Lift the paver and remove the bracket. Then, line up the bracket with the mark on the frame and secure it to the frame with deck screws (photo O). Replace the paver, and reach underneath with a bolt and washer to secure the bracket to the paver. The pavers inside the perimeter do not need to be secured—those on the perimeter will hold them in place.

12 The lower level of the deck requires a sand base. This project had sand in place already, since a swimming pool sat in that location previously. Rake the lower deck area level; if not already present, pour a 1-inch sand base to support the pavers, and rake the sand level.

13 Install pavers, tamping them well into place (photo P), and then checking for level. Check subsequent rows of pavers for level by running a 2-foot level or board back and forth across the seams between pavers (photo Q). If the level doesn't hit the edge of the paver, you know the stone is even.

TIPS | DIY Network
Gardening & Landscaping

REMOVING SUPPORT POSTS
To remove any support posts that may remain from an old structure and are not needed for the new deck, either dig out the post, or wrap it with a chain and pull it out using a compact utility loader.

◢ BUILDING A COPPER COUNTERTOP ◣

The frame for this counter is built from boards salvaged from the old deck, wrapped in copper sheeting, and secured with screws. It's a great multi-use surface for entertaining and grilling on the deck.

You Will Need

- Salvaged posts and planks from decking
- Reciprocating saw
- 2½-3" galvanized or coated decking screws
- Drill and bits
- Circular saw
- Copper sheeting
- Tin snips or electric metal shears
- Tape measure
- Safety goggles and gloves
- Mallet

1 Create built-in support for the counter by using beams left intact from the previous deck, cut to counter height above the new paver deck surface. Cut remaining needed legs from salvaged posts to support the rest of the counter on the deck surface.

2 Mark and cut salvaged decking planks to frame the counter. Attach the planks to the leg posts with screws, creating the frame for the countertop (photo A).

3 Cut additional planks to length for the top of the counter and secure them to the frame with screws as well.

4 Wrap a length of copper sheeting across the width of the counter (photo B). Cut the sheeting to size with tin snips or electric metal shears. Leaving an overhang of several inches at the head of the counter to wrap the top edge of the planks, secure the short edge of the copper underneath the frame with screws (photo C). Always wear gloves when working with copper or any kind of metal sheeting.

5 Bend the copper across the countertop using a mallet to mold it to the frame (photo D), and attach it on the other side of the frame.

6 Cover the rest of the counter in the same manner, overlapping the previous sheet slightly (photo E). Finish the edges by cutting 45-degree angles at the corners and bending the copper over the edge of the top planks, securing it with screws.

FINISHING TOUCHES

Construct a cedar planter box for the deck to accent the paver colors, and plant tall trees such as techny arborvitae and thornless honey locust around the deck for additional privacy.

ALL-WEATHER RENOVATION

Julie owns a home in Los Angeles and her back yard can't handle the moisture from rain and runoff. She built her own deck with a canopy over it, hoping to put in a hot tub and have a dog-friendly yard, but, in the last year, the deck has become weather-worn and the screws are pushing out. In addition, the short distance from the back door to the deck is often muddy—a mess for shoes and paws alike. *Grounds for Improvement* Landscape Designer Dean Hill developed a solution to dry out the backyard and bring it back to life.

■ **PROJECT SUMMARY** ■

Dean Hill and Jackie Taylor helped Julie solve the moisture problem in her yard with a track drain. They also rebuilt the deck with weather-proof (and dog-proof) composite decking, and laid a flagstone path connecting the house to the deck. With new plantings to spruce it up as well, this backyard became a natural choice for enjoying the outdoors—rain or shine!

BEFORE: Patchy grass and muddy spots were the norm in this backyard due to inadequate drainage.

AFTER: Once the track drains were installed near the house, the rest of the yard could be beautified with other weather-resistant additions like the pathway and composite deck.

◣ INSTALLING A TRACK DRAIN ◢

Before implementing any drainage solution, consider the sources of your water problem—in the case of this house, the issues were surface drainage from a sloping yard and roof runoff from the downspout. A modular track drainage system collects moisture and uses gravity to direct and disperse it away. The tracks used to collect the water are made of PVC pipe. The pipes that disperse the water are ABS material, which is sometimes used for sewer lines.

You Will Need

Modular track drainage system	Metal edging
Spade	Mallet or hammer
Shovel	Landscaping fabric
Painter's tape	Gravel
Reciprocating saw	

1 Dig a trench about 12 inches deep on the high end (photo A), and sloping gradually down on the low end. Dropping ⅛ - ½ inch every 10 feet should be a great enough incline. Gravity will do the work of carrying the water down the incline of the track, out of the problem area. In this case, the crew needed to expose the buried lines of the sprinkler system to be able to work carefully around them (photo B).

2 Lay the track in place to check the elevation of the trench (photo C). Snap a cover on the end piece at the start of the track, and use couplers to connect additional tracks for the length needed. The track kit also includes 90-degree-angle segments to create corners if necessary (photo D).

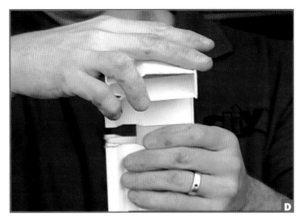

3 Tape over the coupler holes before laying the track in place in order to keep the dirt out as you work (photo E). Then, position the track in the trench.

4 Use a reciprocating saw to cut a small piece of ABS pipe (photo F). Connect it to a 90-degree joint, and add a longer run of pipe (photo G). Cut additional pieces of pipe for another 90-degree angle, and then add the spout and drain cover that come with the kit (photo H).

5 After the track is laid and angled properly, backfill over the ABS pipe in the trench (photo I). Also backfill the trench around the drainage track, leaving the track exposed.

6 Install metal edging to create a border for the gravel. Use a mallet to secure the spikes, provided with the edging, through the joints into the soil.

7 Remove the protective tape that covers the holes on the drainage track (photo J). Lay landscaping cloth over the soil and track to prevent weeds from growing up and to keep the gravel from sinking down (photo K). Use spikes or sod staples to secure the landscaping cloth.

8 Fill in the trench with gravel (photo L)--any grade will work. Choose one with a look you like in your yard. Smooth out the gravel, keeping it contained within the border and even with the sidewalk.

◄ INSTALLING COMPOSITE DECKING ►

Remove the existing planks from your deck and reuse the framing and structure to rebuild it. In this project, the crew strengthened the joists to hold a hot tub--a potential 3,000 pounds of dead weight--and redecked the frame with composite boards. These boards require no maintenance, have no splinters or knots, and will wear much longer than using a wood product underfoot.

You Will Need

Drill	2" galvanized or coated decking screws
Circular saw	Tape measure
¾" x 6" to ⁵⁄₄" x 6" composite decking	Chalk line

1 To remove your existing decking, use a drill in reverse to back out the deck screws, or a crow bar or hammer to remove nails. Then lift out the boards.

2 Reuse the decking boards by cutting them to size for blocking between the deck joists. The blocking will strengthen the deck and keep the joists from flexing under the weight of a hot tub. Secure the blocking with decking screws (photo A).

3 Install the new composite decking, allowing the planks to hang over the edge of the frame on one end by 2 inches (photo B). Using a screw as a spacer between boards, secure them to the joists, driving two deck screws into each joist.

4 Use a chalk line to mark the edge of the deck boards for trimming to a 2-inch overhang. Cut along the chalk line with a circular saw to finish the edge (photo C).

LAYING A FLAGSTONE PATH

Flagstones are flat pavers that often have irregular edges and are usually made from sandstone, limestone, or slate. They need to be set on a level surface, or they will break. A flagstone path is an attractive way to break up long stretches of sod—or mud—and create a connection between your house or walkway and the resurfaced deck.

You Will Need

Spade	Flagstones
Metal edging with spikes	Landscaping fabric
Mallet	Spikes or sod staples
Metal hack saw or reciprocating saw	Gravel

1 Use a spade to cut the outline for the flagstone path (photo A) to a depth that allows the metal edging to stand ½ to 1 inch above the ground.

2 Install metal edging into the cut with a mallet and spikes provided by the manufacturer (photo B). Use a metal hack saw to cut the edging to size. (photo C).

3 Smooth over the soil in the pathway for a level surface to support the flagstones (photo D). Cover the soil with landscaping fabric. Secure it with spikes or sod staples. The fabric will prevent weeds from growing up between the flagstones and also keep smaller gravel from sinking into the ground.

4 Set and level the flagstones on the pathway. When laying flagstone, consider your natural walking stride--set the stones so your foot lands squarely on a flagstone when you take a natural step.

5 Fill around the flagstones with gravel (photo E), being sure to cover every inch of landscape fabric (photo F). Rake or smooth the gravel even with the top of the flagstones.

E

FINISHING TOUCHES

Use extra composite decking boards to make step tiles or a platform for underneath a chair swing (photo at right). Install new plantings along the walkway and near  the deck, using a layer of bark mulch on top to keep moisture in and give a rich look to the area.

F

4

Outdoor Play

The projects in this chapter are the ultimate in personalizing your backyard! Instead of spending your hobby time away from home, make home the ideal place for your hobbies. In this chapter, you'll see how possible it is. If you're an oyster lover, a golf fanatic, or have a penchant for a good game of horseshoes, this chapter brings it home. Or if you aren't, it just may inspire you pursue another style of play space for your own dream yard.

Dave   *Jackie*

PERSONAL PUTTING GREEN

Sam and Lee's children are in their teens, so a yard with weeds and a rusty swingset does them little good. Lee and his daughter Katie love to golf, so *Grounds for Improvement's* Dean Hill and Jackie Taylor developed a design that would allow them to golf right in their own backyard.

◀ PROJECT SUMMARY ▶

Jackie Taylor and Dean Hill showed Sam and Lee how to install their own putting green, complete with a sand trap tailored to the level of difficulty they wanted. The crew also put in a seating area for spectators.

BEFORE: No one in this family was using the old swingset anymore. It was time for a place the kids could entertain their friends and spend time with the family (above).

AFTER: A personal putting green and ring-side bunker was just the ticket for this family. A neglected backyard has become the focal point of free time.

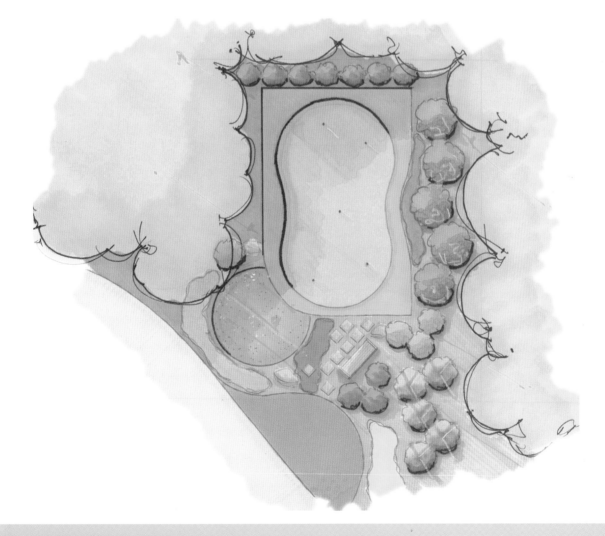

◢◢◢ **INSTALLING A PUTTING GREEN** ◣◣◣

Putting greens come in one piece, completely put together—no seams to match or holes to cut. The grass used in this project is rectangular, made from a nylon material with a synthetic rubber foam base. These types of putting greens come in all shapes and sizes, including rectangles, kidney shapes, and strips. Rent a compact utility loader to make short work of preparing the base for the green, and a plate compactor to tamp the gravel courses.

You Will Need	
Shovels	2.3 tons of fine crushed gravel
Rakes	17' x 23' rectangular putting green
Wheelbarrow	Sod staples or landscape spikes
Compact utility loader	Hammer or mallet
Landscape marking paint	Utility knife
Tape measure	5 putting green cups
5.5 tons of gravel	Trowel
Plate compactor	

1 Clear any plant growth away and level the ground with a compact utility loader (photo A). If rainwater washes through the area from other parts of the yard, be sure that the sub-base surface slopes slightly away to allow adequate drainage.

2 Measure and mark out the area for the putting green using landscape paint (photo B). The fringe of the putting green can be cut later to fit snugly to any perimeter landscaping.

3 After the dimensions are outlined, begin installing the gravel base. Pour gravel onto the sub-base with wheelbarrows and rake it evenly (photo C). Tamp it down with a rented plate compactor making several passes. This makes tamping a cinch, and it can be rented by the day. Make sure to level any uneven spots with a rake or shovel so that water will not pool on the green.

4 Next, put down a layer of very fine limestone gravel (photo D). This acts as a leveling course, increases the drainage, and also protects the putting green from the harder gravel below, so rocks underneath do not affect the roll of the ball. This layer also allows you to make any desired dips, movement, or bunkering of the green to create a more challenging course. Tamp down this layer with the plate compactor with several passes as well (photo E).

5 Roll out the putting green carefully over the gravel course, avoiding stepping on the compacted gravel. The best way to do this is to position helpers on both ends of the green, lifting up the the edges of the green to position it as though positioning a bed sheet, "billowing" it into place (photo F).

6 Secure the perimeter of the green using sod staples or landscape spikes. Separate the fibers on the fringe to drive a staple or spike through the mat into the gravel below. Anchor it about every 6-8 inches, pulling the turf as you work along one side—as though pulling carpet.

7 Use a utility blade to carefully trim the fringe of the putting green to fit around any pre-existing shrubs.

8 Next, install the holes and cups. The putting green comes with holes pre-cut into the turf. Loosen the gravel through the hole in the green with a hand trowel and carefully remove it by hand. Set the cups in the holes, making sure each is level with the turf, no higher, so the cup does not impede the ball in play (photo G).

TIPS DIY Network
Gardening & Landscaping

PUTTING GREEN BASE

You can also use the fine limestone gravel as the base for the putting green, but the larger gravel underneath offers a sturdier surface for the green.

▶ BUILDING A SAND TRAP ◀

No putting green is complete without a ring-side bunker. Tailor this sand trap to offer a greater challenge by adjusting the depth and shape you dig the base—from a shallow bowl to a base dug a foot deep for a greater challenge. You can buy bunker sand from most golf courses or find a resource that sells it directly. Be sure to purchase a little extra sand to refill the sand trap as needed.

You Will Need

Pruning shears or hand saw	Landscaping fabric
Landscape marking paint	Landscape spikes
Shovels and spades	2 tons of bunker sand
Wheelbarrow	Aluminum edging and stakes
Base gravel	Hammer or mallet

1 Cut back any tree branches over the bunker area that might impede ball flight out of the bunker, and mark out the area for the sand bunker next to the putting green using landscape paint.

2 Remove any brush or sod from the area with shovels. Then choose the depth and shape of your sand trap, and dig out the trap (photo A).

TIPS | DIY Network Gardening & Landscaping

CARE OF YOUR SAND TRAP
Rotate the sand in your bunker on rainy days, or use a tarp to keep it dry. With a sand trap 1 foot deep or less, water pooling up in the sand should not be an issue. Cover the bunker whenever it's not in use to keep pets out of the sand.

3 Spread a layer of base gravel over the dirt, raking it evenly across (photo B). Then lay down landscaping fabric, which will keep the sand in place, prevent weeds, and allow for drainage. Secure the weed barrier with landscape spikes across the fabric (photo C).

4 Fill the bunker sand over the landscape fabric and spread it evenly (photo D). Make sure not to overfill the bunker initially, and keep it firm enough that your feet do not sink into the sand.

5 Finally, enclose the sand bunker with metal edging to keep the sand contained. Secure the edging with stakes provided (photo E).

FINISHING TOUCHES

Discard the largest clumps of dirt and roots from the pile of soil created by clearing the area for the green. Rake the rest of the soil evenly over the ground, and cover it with mulch. Install plants on the fringe of the putting green, and add a layer of mulch to the flower beds. Lay paver stones for a walking path and place a bench with a strategic vantage point to watch the players practice their strokes!

TIPS | DIY Network Gardening & Landscaping

REMOVING A SWING SET

To remove an old swing set, cut the supporting bars with a reciprocating saw to remove the bulk of the structure. Then, use a compact utility loader to drag out or push out the swing posts.

HORSESHOE PLATFORMS

Dusty has a large lot with a narrow creek running right down the middle. He has a party pavilion for entertaining, but nothing else in his vast yard. The only way to get over the creek is to jump and risk falling in. So *Grounds for Improvement* Landscape Designer Dean Hill created a solution to put a bridge over troubled waters and install horseshoe platforms for Dusty's party guests to enjoy a little friendly competition.

BEFORE: This yard had plenty of space, but that was it. Not a lot of interest, and the yard was cut in half by a stream.

◀ PROJECT SUMMARY ▶

In this project, the *Grounds for Improvement* team Dean Hill and Jackie Taylor showed Dusty how to build horseshoe pits next to his outdoor pavilion for he and his friends to enjoy. They built a redwood bridge across the creek, creating an attractive, practical way to cross the water, and a gravel path between the playing field and the bridge to connect the areas.

AFTER: With an attractive bridge and stone pathway connecting the yard, this space takes on a whole new demeanor with a game of horseshoes ready and waiting.

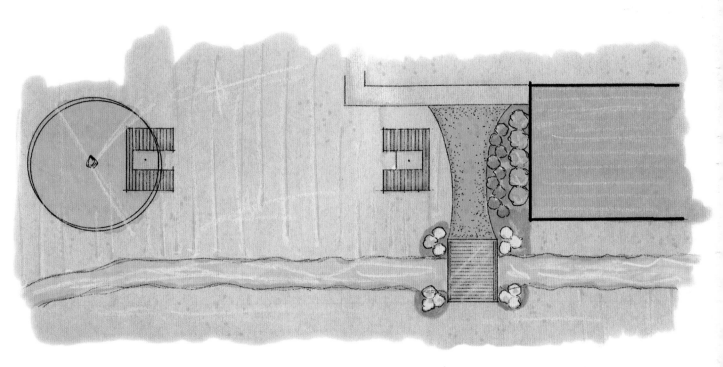

◣ BUILDING THE PLATFORMS ◢

Regulation horseshoe pits are 40 feet apart, stake to stake, so select an area with plenty of room for the game and space for onlookers too. These horseshoe pits have a pitching platform and a drink ledge. Use pressure-treated lumber for the wood that will sit directly on the ground and composite lumber for the decking.

You Will Need

Tape measure and pencil	(4) 1¼" x 6" x 10' composite decking
Landscape marking paint	(24) 1¼" x 6" x 8' composite decking
Flat shovels	#5 box 2" deck screws
Wheelbarrows	(4) 4" x 4" x 8' pressure-treated posts
Miter saw	5" bolts with nuts
Safety goggles and gloves	Regulation horseshoe set
Cordless screwdriver	Mallet
(4) 2" x 6" x 10' pressure-treated timbers	Hand tamp
(18) 2" x 6" x 8' pressure-treated timbers	Circular saw

1 Determine the area for your playing field, measuring 40 feet between the horseshoe pits. Use landscape marking paint to mark out the areas for the platforms and the pits that will be in the middle (photo A). The pitching platforms are each about 8 feet wide, recessed in the ground 1 to 2 inches. The pit within the platform is 18 inches from outer lip to stake and 36 inches wide.

2 Use flat shovels to remove sod and a small amount of soil in the marked area (photo B), hauling away the dirt and sod with wheelbarrows. These shallow trenches will hold the pitching platform frames.

3 Measure and mark the 2x6 pressure-treated lumber for cutting (photo C). The outside of the platform frames are 7-feet long, and the inside boards are 64 inches. Use a miter saw to cut the boards (photo D). Cut the 1¼x6 composite lumber with the miter saw as well—cutting 48 boards to 38 inches long. Always wear gloves and safety goggles when cutting.

4 Lay out the cut boards to assemble the horseshoe pit frames before moving them into place (photo E). Attach the boards with 2-inch deck screws.

5 Measure, cut, and install support pieces between the boards of the frame as well (photo F).

LUMBER CHOICES

Pressure-treated lumber is designed to withstand rotting, so it's well-suited to outdoor uses and contact with soil. Composite lumber is not wood—it's made from recycled plastic grocery bags and other materials. Composite lumber has no knot holes or raised grain and doesn't produce splinters, so it's a great choice for decking. Both pressure-treated lumber and composite decking are available at most home improvement stores.

6 Move the assembled frame into place (photo G), using several people to lift and carry it. Check it for level, filling in with soil below as needed. No spikes or cement are necessary to keep the platform in place, the weight of the platform is sufficient.

7 Lay the composite decking boards in place on the frame. Predrill holes through the decking and attach the boards with 2-inch deck screws (photo H).

8 Attach 4x4 pressure-treated timbers as support posts for the backstop. Drill through the posts and frame and secure the posts with bolts, checking for level and plumb. Screw composite decking boards onto the backstop posts (photo I) for a finished look.

9 Attach a pressure-treated board to the top of the posts for a beverage shelf. Cut scrap wood into right-angle triangle supports for a second shelf on the back of the backstop (photo J).

10 Install a board across the front of the horseshoe pit to mark the lip of the play area (photo K). Then fill the pit from the lip to the pitching platform with dirt. Use a hand tamp to firm the soil.

11 Install the horseshoe rod 2 feet from the lip of the frame and 18 inches from each side of the platform. Use a mallet to tap the rod into the ground, and make sure it is angled toward the other platform (photo L). The rod should extend exactly 14 inches above the ground (photo M).

CUTTING EQUAL-LENGTH BOARDS

To cut multiple boards to the same length on a miter saw, attach a "stopper" to the miter saw table with clamps. Create the stopper by nailing two boards into a T. At the intersection of the boards, attach a shorter board that, when clamped to the miter saw table, is exactly the needed length from the saw blade (photo below). Then, each board butted against the stopper will be cut at uniform length.

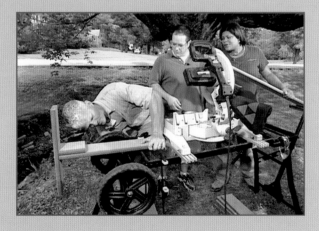

BUILDING A REDWOOD BRIDGE

This flat bridge is simple construction with posts anchored into the ground, a spread beam on top of the posts, and joists between the beams with redwood decking on top. The strong and naturally weatherproof redwood boards add a great look to any yard. The bridge is 10 feet long with support posts 8 feet apart underneath. To determine the length for your bridge, look at the dimensions of the bank. The support posts need to be far enough onto the bank that you can dig postholes below the frost line for your region.

You Will Need

Landscape marking paint	#5 box 3" deck screws
Tape measure and pencil	Cordless screwdriver
Posthole diggers	1 box 8" timber spikes
Wheelbarrow	Sledge hammer
(6) 6" x 6" x 8' pressure-treated timbers	(9) 4" x 6" x 10' pressure-treated timbers
Chainsaw	Shovels
4' level	(20) 2" x 6" x 8' redwood boards
12 bags of quick-set concrete	Drill and bits
Water source and hose or buckets	

1 Mark out the area for the 6 support posts with landscape marking paint (photo A), measuring 8 feet between them across the stream. On each side of the stream, three posts will support the bridge. One support post will line up with each edge of the gravel path, and one will align with the center of the path.

2 Use a posthole digger to dig the holes as marked (photo B). Haul the soil away with a wheelbarrow.

3 Mark 6x6 posts for cutting to length for your region, 10-inch lengths in this project (photo C), and make the cuts with a chainsaw (photo D).

4 Set the posts in place in their holes (photo E). Lay a long board across all three posts in order to check them for level (photo F). Adjust the soil beneath the posts as necessary to achieve level.

TIPS DIY Network
Gardening & Landscaping

CHAINSAW SAFETY

Before running your chainsaw, make sure the chain is sharpened and has enough oil. Use the length of the saw, not the tip, for cutting so the chain won't grab or pop off. Let the saw do the work.

5 Secure the posts in the holes using quick-set concrete mix and water (photo G). The concrete will set in about 20 to 40 minutes. Heavy objects can be attached to the posts after 4 hours.

6 For this project, before the concrete set completely, the crew put the 6x6 crossbeams in place, rechecked for level, and secured the crossbeams to the posts by driving 3-inch deck screws in at an angle (photo H).

7 After the concrete is set, drive 8-inch timber spikes through the crossbeams into the support posts.

8 Run 4x6 pressure-treated joists from one side of the creek to the other (photo I). In this project, additional soil was removed to make room for the joists extending over the cross beams so the surface of the bridge was at ground level.

9 Secure the joists to the crossbeams with 8-inch timber spikes (photo J). To add additional support, secure them with 3-inch deck screws driven in at an angle as well.

10 With the joists in place, lay down the 2x6 redwood decking. Predrill holes on the decking into the joists, and secure the boards with decking screws (photo K).

11 Attach a pressure-treated board to each side of the bridge with decking screws to serve as a curb (photo L).

TIPS
DIY Network
Gardening & Landscaping

HAMMERING TIMBER SPIKES

The task of hammering timber spikes is easier if you drive them in at an angle toward you. If you are right handed, hold the sledge hammer with your right hand forward, and vice versa for left-handers or whatever is most comfortable for you. Let the weight of the sledge hammer do the work, allowing it to fall onto the spike.

◼ INSTALLING A GRAVEL PATH ◼

This project is a simple way to connect two areas of your yard—in this case, the redwood bridge and the horseshoe platforms. Use pea gravel contained on the path by metal edging. Materials listed are for a 24-foot path.

You Will Need

Landscape marking paint	Landscape spikes
Tape measure	Wheelbarrows
Flat shovels	Shovels
(6) 8' sections of metal edging with hardware	1 ton pea gravel
200 square feet landscaping fabric	Rakes

1 Mark out the edges for the gravel path with landscape marking paint. In this project, the path was 4 feet wide in the center, fanning out equally at each end to the width of the bridge.

2 Remove the sod from the area of the path with flat shovels (photo A). Install metal edging along each side of the path to hold the gravel. Secure the edging with the spikes provided by the manufacturer and a mallet or hammer (photo B).

TIPS
DIY Network
Gardening & Landscaping

GRAVEL DELIVERY

When your gravel is delivered, have it poured on a large tarp near the site for the walkway. This will minimize heavy wheelbarrow work and allow for easy clean-up later.

3 Cover the pathway with landscaping fabric to prevent weeds from growing up in the stone yet allow drainage. Secure the fabric with landscape spikes every 18 inches or so.

4 Haul gravel in wheelbarrows to fill the path and rake it out evenly within the edging (photo C).

FINISHING TOUCHES

Install plantings along the walkway and set potted flowers around the horseshoe pit platforms. Day lilies make a lovely accent along the bridge by the water. A volleyball net and a croquet course can quickly add to the party options for your yard as well.

LOW COUNTRY GRILL

Anna and Dennis' home in the low-country of Charleston, South Carolina, is situated next to a tidal marsh. Between the marsh and their yard is a wooded area that is vital to the health of the waterways. This "buffer zone," however, is not very inviting for their kids. Following Dean Hill's design and with Jackie Taylor's help, the couple and their friends spend two days turning the buffer zone into an attractive area for the whole family, while still protecting the foliage.

◤ PROJECT SUMMARY ◢

After building a gravel path from the back deck to the buffer area, and planting some large trees to create subtle separation and privacy from the neighbor's yard, the homeowners and the *Grounds for Improvement* team build a freestanding oyster-roasting pit. To finish it off, they add beautiful planting beds with mulch and a variety of local shrubs.

BEFORE: The pine-filled buffer between the house and the tidal marsh offered space for the family to enjoy its backyard, but a small fire pit and a play set weren't making the most of this natural space.

AFTER: The oyster roasting pit gives the family a place to enjoy time together and to entertain guests. And now, a bit of pine straw cover, new plantings, and a winding path to the deck make the buffer zone an inviting place.

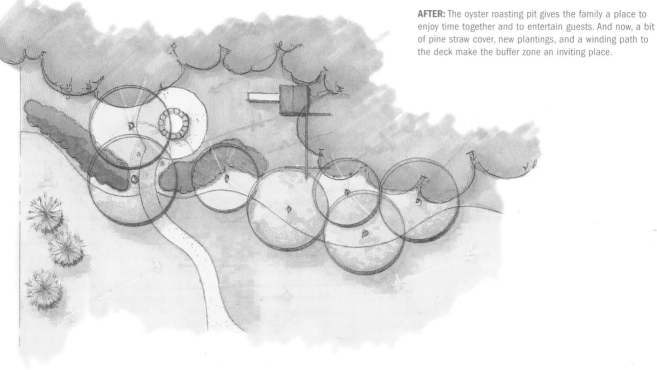

TIPS | DIY Network
Gardening & Landscaping

MAKING A PATH

Design a flowing path with arcs rather than sharp curves or angles. Nice gentle sweeps will make a more attractive path for your yard.

CREATING A GRAVEL PATH

This gravel path is 3 feet wide, the recommended minimum width for a walking path. Landscaping fabric under the path prevents the gravel from sinking into the ground, allows water to drain through, and prevents weeds from growing up through the gravel. Aluminum edging helps keep the gravel in place and provides an edge for mowing or trimming. You will need to rent a plate compactor for this project to set the gravel firmly in place.

You Will Need

Landscape marking paint	Aluminum edging stakes
Tape measure	280 square feet landscaping fabric
Sod cutter	Spikes or sod staples
Shovels	Mallet
Spades	4 cubic yards of small gravel
Wheelbarrows	Rakes
128 linear feet aluminum edging	Plate compactor

1 Mark out the area for the gravel path with landscape marking paint (photo A). When one side of the path is marked, use a tape measure to mark the 3-foot width every few feet of the path. Then, connect these marks with paint (photo B).

2 Use a sod cutter to cut out the area for the walkway (photo C). A sod cutter can be rented by the day and will save you a lot of manual labor. Use spades and shovels to loosen the sod after it is cut, then roll up the cut pieces (photo D) and haul them off in wheelbarrows.

3 Install the edging, which will keep the gravel from spilling out of the path and provide an edge for mowing or trimming. Dig a narrow, 6-inch-deep trench on both sides of the path for the edging. It will rest ½ inch to 1 inch above the ground. Secure each section, driving stakes through the slots on the edging and into the ground. Inserting the stakes in each section before bending it to form the path makes the job much easier (photo E).

4 Next, lay down landscaping fabric on the path. Secure the fabric with spikes or sod staples.

5 Spread the gravel over the filter fabric (photo F), and rake it out evenly. Go over the path several times with the plate compactor to set the gravel firmly for a good walking surface (photo G).

◀ BUILDING AN OYSTER PIT ▶

This oyster pit has a 4-foot-diameter opening and spans 6 feet altogether. It is made of concrete block, four courses (or rows) high, with the fourth course comprised of concrete caps. These blocks weigh roughly 35 pounds each and stand 4 inches tall, the same kind often used for retaining walls. You will need to rent a plate compactor for this project.

You Will Need

Landscape marking paint	Concrete cut-off saw with a diamond tipped blade
Tape measure	Water source
2' rebar or stake	Wheelbarrow
Hammer or mallet	Broom or brush
Small gravel	6 tubes of paver bond
2x4 board	20 "A" concrete caps in brown/charcoal blend
4' level	Wax pencil or carpenter's pencil
Rake	16-20 standard fire bricks
Hand tamp	4' diameter grates for roasting
80 concrete-block accent units in brown/charcoal blend	Plate compactor
Sledge hammer	

1 Mark the center point of the pit using landscape marking paint. Holding one end of the tape measure in the center of the pit, circle around, marking the outside perimeter of the pit as well (photo A). Then, drive a piece of rebar or a stake into the center of the circle as a point of reference. (The stake needs to be able to withstand gravel pouring over it.)

2 Spread a layer of base gravel over the circle and rake it out evenly. Both the center and the ring under the block wall need a gravel base. Use a 2x4 and a level to get an even base (photo B), and then tamp out any sections that need extra attention with a hand tamp (photo C).

3 Next, install the first course, or row, of block. Measure and mark out 2 feet from the center stake around the circle with landscape marking paint to create the 4-foot-diameter inner circle. Then lay the first course of block. As you place each block, level it front to back and then side to side using a level and a sledge hammer to make adjustments (photo D). Spending the time to make sure each block is level will prevent problems on each subsequent course. Use a concrete cut-off saw to cut the final block in the circle to size, wetting the block as you saw to reduce dust (photo E).

4 Pour gravel around the perimeter of the oyster pit, and also inside the pit, before the walls go higher (photo F). Sweep away any loose debris on top of the first course. Use a plate compactor or hand tamp to tamp down the gravel outside the pit.

5 Then, dry fit the second course, placing blocks to overlap the joints from the

previous layer. Dry fit the entire second course to ensure that every piece fits properly.

6 When the second course is laid, lift the blocks, one by one, and apply concrete adhesive underneath (photo G, next page). No need to wait for the blocks to dry from cutting—the concrete adhesive will work on wet blocks.

7 Repeat steps 5 and 6 for the third course of block.

8 Then, begin to lay the course of caps. Caps are made of the same high-strength concrete as the wall blocks, but do not have the interlocking slits. To add the caps, first lay cap blocks over each joint of the third course, spacing them evenly apart (photo H, next page). Cut blocks will be placed between the whole blocks in the next steps. This method keeps the outer face of the wall consistent, without edges jutting out.

TIPS | DIY Network
Gardening & Landscaping

BLOCK SUPPORT
Concrete adhesive is sufficient for a wall of this height. For higher walls, you can insert pins through the slits in the blocks to secure the pieces together.

9 Mark the caps for cutting that will fit between the whole caps that have been set in place. To do this, center one block cap on top of those which it will fit between when cut. Use a pencil to mark the underside along the edges where the top block overlaps the blocks underneath (photo I). Mark both front and back edges. Flip the marked block over and use a straight-edge or level to connect the marks for the cutting lines.

10 Use a wax pencil to number the block and the space in which it will fit as well, since not all of the blocks will be cut uniformly. The wax markings will not come off during the wet cutting of the block as pencil may.

11 Cut the marked concrete caps to size, wetting the block as you cut. Put them in place between the first caps laid. Use concrete adhesive to secure this layer in the same manner as before.

12 To create a "stand" for the grate, place four stacks of fire bricks around the inside of the oyster pit, using four or five bricks per stack (photo J). Be sure to use fire brick as it has a high tolerance for extreme temperatures and will hold up well in a fire pit.

13 Set the grate directly on top of the fire brick, and place an additional mesh grate on top for oyster roasting. These grates are lifted out to set the fire beneath. For easier access, install a hinged grate on the pit instead.

INSTALLING LARGE TREES

In this project, bald cypress trees were installed—a very adaptable and hardy tree that loves water, so it was well-suited to the marsh location of this project.

You Will Need

Shovels	3 burlap-balled bald cypress trees
Spades	Pine straw
Scrap sheet of plywood	Water source
Tape measure	

1 Dig a hole twice as wide and just as deep as the rootball of the tree. Transfer the soil onto a sheet of plywood temporarily to prevent making a mess in the yard.

2 Remove the tree from its container and note the top of the rootball and the top of the crown—the area that extends out from the base of the trunk above the bulk of dirt. Place the tree in the hole so that the top of the rootball is at ground level (photo A).

3 If the tree is covered with soil to its crown, it will not get the oxygen it needs. So, be careful to backfill the hole with soil only to the top of the rootball (photo B). Then cover the soil loosely with pine straw mulch, including the top of the rootball to the crown. The mulch will help keep in moisture, yet also let in oxygen. Haul the remaining sod away on the board.

FINISHING TOUCHES

Planting beds were made by removing the sod and planting native shrubs such as pink muhly grass, sweet pepperbush, Shenandoah switch grass, Virginia sweetspire and other perennials along the gravel path, with pine straw for mulch.

APPENDIX: PLANTING TIPS

One of the most important aspects of landscaping is knowing when and how to plant all of the flowers, shrubs, and trees you've chosen for your yard, and how to care for them after they are in the ground. The following tips will help guide you in the planting process so your new yard can be a stunning success.

Flowers are one of the easiest ways to add splashes of color and personality to your outdoor living spaces.

Flowers can be grown at home from seeds, or purchased at nurseries as seedlings, young plants, or full-grown plants.

To grow plants from seed, simply plant the seeds at the depth and spacing suggested on the package, then cover with a loose layer of plastic and place in a sunny spot. Keep the soil moist, as directed on the package.

Seedlings are a fun way to buy plants in bulk. If you choose to order seedlings through the mail, be sure to unwrap them as soon as they arrive and test the soil for moisture. Water as often as necessary and keep in a sunny location until you're ready to plant.

Young and full-grown plants can be planted immediately, although you may want to give them a few days to acclimate to their new environment if they'll be moving from a warm greenhouse to cooler temperatures. Take extra care not to damage their roots as you remove them from trays and to water them frequently.

◄ PLANTING TREES ►

Planting and nurturing trees is a rewarding way to add shade, privacy and visual appeal to your yard.

Choose a planting site with the size of your future tree in mind, allowing as much space and sun as suggested by the grower.

Seedlings. If you start with a seedling it's important to chose an area protected from wind if possible. To prepare the planting site, turn the soil and remove any nearby weeds whose roots would absorb water that will be needed by the seedling.

Ideally, seedlings should be planted within two days of delivery. If you can't plant your seedlings right away, cover its roots with loose, moist soil.

Keep the soil moist until you're ready to plant. If you've purchased multiple seedlings in trays, place the whole tray in water for ten minutes to soak the roots, then cover the seedlings with loose soil.

To begin planting, stir a shovelful of dirt into a bucket half-filled with water. Place the seedlings in the bucket, taking care to submerge their roots.

Next, dig a round hole at least one foot in diameter. Create a small mound of soil in the bottom of hole and place the seedling in the hole. Gently spread the roots out in all directions. Use the small mound as support for the roots. Sprinkle loose soil over the roots until you've filled half of the hole, then fill the remaining space in the hole with water. After the water is absorbed, fill the rest of the hole with soil, lightly tamp, and water again. Remember: always tamp the soil lightly; packing the soil too tightly removes oxygen that the roots need. The seedling's root collar should be resting at the finished soil level.

Water your newly planted seedlings as often as needed to keep the soil most. You can check moisture by digging up a small amount of soil near your seedling to feed the soil below the surface. A layer of mulch is a great way to maintain soil moisture and discourage weed growth.

Potted Trees. If you've purchased a potted tree, hold the base of the main stem and gently pull with one hand while pushing up on the soil from the bottom of the pot with your other hand. Take extra care to keep the root ball intact. Do not leave root balls exposed to sun or wind before planting. Dig a hole twice as wide as the root ball and just as deep. Follow the instructions for backfilling and watering the hole as for seedlings above. If you're planting a potted tree, double-check that no root surfaces are exposed to the air after watering.

◣ PLANTING SHRUBS ▶

Shrubs are sold in three forms: bare root, balled and burlapped, and container grown.

Bare-root shrubs are the most economical choice and are best planted in early spring or winter. To plant, dig a hole twice as large as the roots; mold a loose cone of soil at the bottom of the hole; set the shrub in the hole, spreading the roots around the cone; backfill the hole halfway; give the plant a good soaking; and fill with remaining soil.

Balled-and-burlapped shrubs and container shrubs are more expensive than bare-root plants, but they're available during the peak gardening season. When selecting a balled-and-burlapped plant, make sure the root ball feels firm to the touch. Loosen and remove the burlap before planting—which may not be easy if the roots have grown into the fabric. To plant, dig a hole twice as large as the root ball and about as deep. Lower the root ball into the hole and center it.

If the shrub is wrapped in plastic or growing in a container, remove the plastic or the container before placing the root ball in the hole. Never lift the plant by the trunk, which may cause the root ball to loosen and fall apart. Always support the roots when lifting them. If the shrub is in a metal container, ask the nursery to cut slits in the can before you take it home so it'll be easier to remove. Remove the can at home before planting.

Backfill the hole as for bare-root plants. The soil should be fine and loose so roots can penetrate it easily. Make sure the top of the root ball is at ground level and the crown—the part of the shrub that extends out from the stem to the rootball—is above ground.

Transplanting Shrubs. Spring and fall are the best times to transplant shrubs from one spot to another.

Use a sharp spade to cut a circle around the roots, then shape the roots and soil into a ball by undercutting the roots. When the ball is free and can be rocked to one side, wrap it in burlap, then fasten with twine to carry it to its new location. Plant as you would a new shrub, and keep the plant cool and moist for two weeks after planting.

Be sure newly planted shrubs receive 1 inch of rain a week during their growing season. In arid climates, build a berm (a ring of mounded soil, which is often mulched) around a newly planted shrub to collect water and aid in watering. Don't use fertilizer until you begin to see new growth. After planting, add a layer of mulch around your new shrubs only ½" deep near the plant but deeper farther from the trunk.

CUSTOM LAWN CHAIR PATTERN

From page 93

All measurements are inches

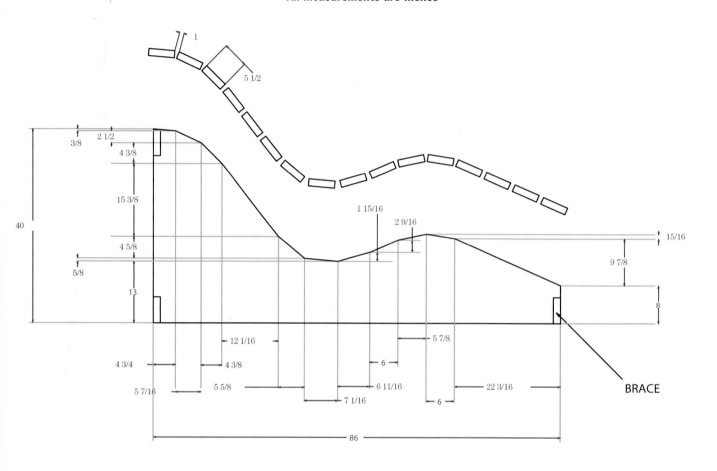

BRACE

METRIC CONVERSION TABLE

Inches	Decimal Inches	Rounded Metric	Inches	Decimal Inches	Rounded Metric	Inches	Decimal Inches	Rounded Metric
1/16	.0625	1.6 mm/.16 cm	7½	7.5	19 cm	18		45.7 cm
1/8	.0125	3 mm/.3 cm	7¾	7.75	19.7 cm	18¼	18.25	46.4 cm
3/16	.1875	5 mm/.5 cm	8		20.3 cm	18½	18.5	47 cm
¼	.25	6 mm/.6 cm	8¼	8.25	21 cm	18¾	18.75	47.6 cm
5/16	.3125	8 mm/.8 cm	8½	8.5	21.6 cm	19		48.3 cm
3/8	.375	9.5 mm/.95 cm	8¾	8.75	22.2 cm	19¼	19.25	48.9 cm
7/16	.4375	1.1 cm	9		22.9 cm	19½	19.5	49.5 cm
½	.5	1.3 cm	9¼	9.25	23.5 cm	19¾	19.75	50.2 cm
9/16	.5625	1.4 cm	9½	9.5	24.1 cm	20		50.8 cm
5/8	.625	1.6 cm	9¾	9.75	24.8 cm	20¼	20.25	51.4 cm
11/16	.6875	1.7 cm	10		25.4 cm	20½	20.5	52.1 cm
¾	.75	1.9 cm	10¼	10.25	26 cm	20¾	20.75	52.7 cm
13/16	.8125	2.1 cm	10½	10.5	26.7 cm	21		53.3 cm
7/8	.875	2.2 cm	10¾	10.75	27.3 cm	21¼	21.25	54 cm
15/16	.9375	2.4 cm	11		27.9 cm	21½	21.5	54.6 cm
			11¼	11.25	28.6 cm	21¾	21.75	55.2 cm
1		2.5 cm	11½	11.5	29.2 cm	22		55.9 cm
1¼	1.25	3.2 cm	11¾	11.75	30 cm	22¼	22.25	56.5 cm
1½	1.5	3.8 cm	12		30.5 cm	22½	22.5	57.2 cm
1¾	1.75	4.4 cm	12¼	12.25	31.1 cm	22¾	22.75	57.8 cm
2		5 cm	12½	12.5	31.8 cm	23		58.4 cm
2¼	2.25	5.7 cm	12¾	12.75	32.4 cm	23¼	23.25	59 cm
2½	2.5	6.4 cm	13		33 cm	23½	23.5	59.7 cm
2¾	2.75	7 cm	13¼	13.25	33.7 cm	23¾	23.75	60.3 cm
3		7.6 cm	13½	13.5	34.3 cm	24		61 cm
3¼	3.25	8.3 cm	13¾	13.75	35 cm	24¼	24.25	61.6 cm
3½	3.5	8.9 cm	14		35.6 cm	24½	24.5	62.2 cm
3¾	3.75	9.5 cm	14¼	14.25	36.2 cm	24¾	24.75	62.9 cm
4		10.2 cm	14½	14.5	36.8 cm	25		63.5 cm
4¼	4.25	10.8 cm	14¾	14.75	37.5 cm	25¼	25.25	64.1 cm
4½	4.5	11.4 cm	15		38.1 cm	25½	25.5	64.8 cm
4¾	4.75	12 cm	15¼	15.25	38.7 cm	25¾	25.75	65.4 cm
5		12.7 cm	15½	15.5	39.4 cm	26		66 cm
5¼	5.25	13.3 cm	15¾	15.75	40 cm	26¼	26.25	66.7 cm
5½	5.5	14 cm	16		40.6 cm	26½	26.5	67.3 cm
5¾	5.75	14.6 cm	16¼	16.25	41.3 cm	26¾	26.75	68 cm
6		15.2 cm	16½	16.5	41.9 cm	27		68.6 cm
6¼	6.25	15.9 cm	16¾	16.75	42.5 cm	27¼	27.25	69.2 cm
6½	6.5	16.5 cm	17		43.2 cm	27½	27.5	69.9 cm
6¾	6.75	17.1 cm	17¼	17.25	43.8 cm	27¾	27.75	70.5 cm
7		17.8 cm	17½	17.5	44.5 cm	28		71.1 cm
7¼	7.25	18.4 cm	17¾	17.75	45.1 cm			

INDEX